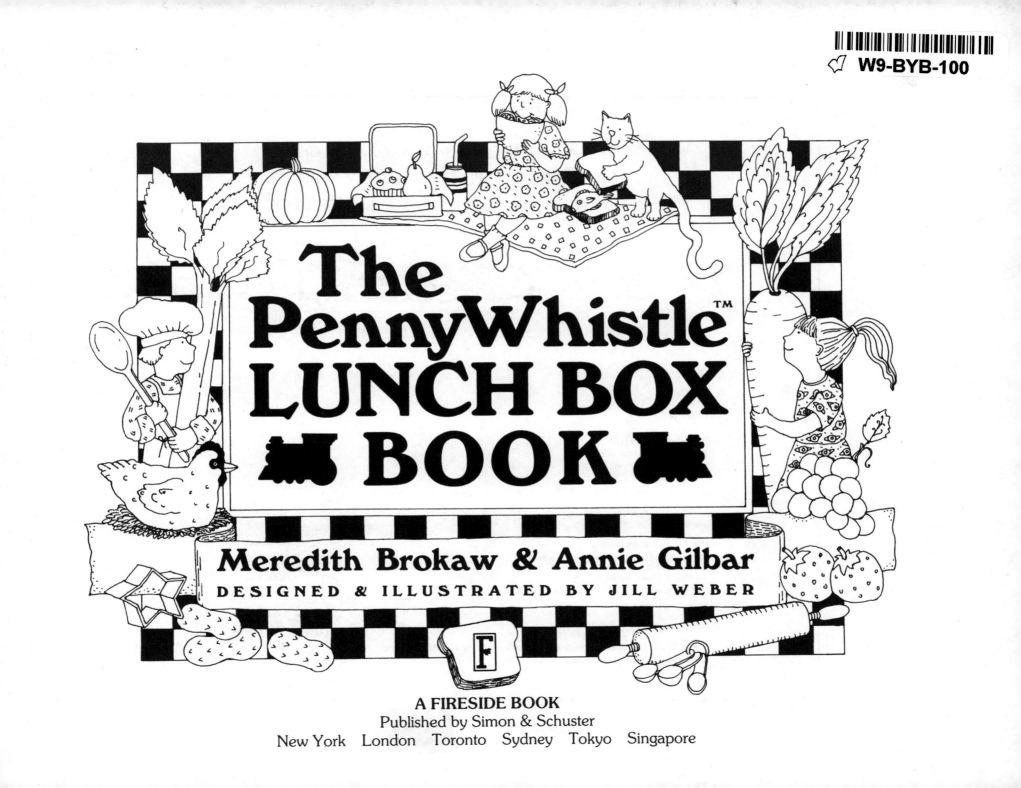

The PennyWhistle™ LUNCH BOX BOOK

Meredith Brokaw & Annie Gilbar

DESIGNED & ILLUSTRATED BY JILL WEBER

A FIRESIDE BOOK
Published by Simon & Schuster
New York   London   Toronto   Sydney   Tokyo   Singapore

Also by Meredith Brokaw and Annie Gilbar

THE PENNY WHISTLE™ PARTY PLANNER

THE PENNY WHISTLE™ HALLOWEEN BOOK

F

FIRESIDE

Rockefeller Center
1230 Avenue of the Americas
New York, New York 10020

First Fireside Edition 1991
Published by arrangement with the authors.

Designed by Jill Weber
Manufactured in the United States of America

10 9 8 7 6 5   Pbk.

ISBN: 0-671-73793-7 Pbk.

Penny Whistle Toys is a registered trademark of Penny Whistle Toys, Inc. and is used herein by permission.

DEDICATION

To all the dedicated mothers and
fathers who make their children's
lunches each and every morning,

And to their children and ours,
who eat them (sometimes).

ACKNOWLEDGMENTS

Thank you, thank you, thank you, to:

Dan Green, Jill Weber, Kathy Robbins, Angela Miller, Janet Surmi, Liz Karatz, Goldine Nicholas, Harriet Ripinsky, Jerry Williams and the people at Epson, the Georgia Peanut Commission and the Peanut Advisory Board,

All the mothers and fathers and many special friends who have so generously shared their ideas and stories,

Our Moms, Esther Ancoli and Vivian Auld, who set the precedent with their loving lunches,

And, as always, Tom Brokaw and Gary Gilbar.

Contents

The Lunch Box Saga

It's a fact of life. Almost every child in this country will, during his or her childhood, take about 1,700 lunch boxes or bags to school, which means we moms and dads will have made most of those 1,700 lunches on 1,700 of those mornings. But take comfort—parents all over the country have been, and are still (some at this very moment), making those peanut butter and jelly sandwiches.

Scenes like these happen daily. Picture this. Tuesday, March 12, 1983, was the 101st consecutive day Annie had made a tuna sandwich on wheat bread, dry, no lettuce or tomato, and put it in her daughter Lisa's lunch box. No one knows why it was that the 101st day, rather than

Veronica Chambers has a new twist on putting a note in your child's lunch box. Her notes are made up of initials (capital letters U R A Q T—you are a cutie; U R G R 8—you are great; etc.). Chris Chambers likes his mom to put other names on his lunch bag. Caesar, Napoleon and Maximilian are favorites. Every now and then, Veronica throws in an unknown name such as Prometheus or Medusa, which makes Chris run to the encyclopedia as soon as he gets home.

the 72nd or the 54th day, got to Annie. All she remembers thinking is—How much longer can I do this? How many more tuna sandwiches on wheat bread, dry, no lettuce or tomato, can I make? Annie decided then and there that the only bearable answer was "none." But that resolution left her with a problem: What was she going to put in that now very empty lunch box?

We should explain the reason Lisa had developed the tuna habit. The first is, simply, that she, like most kids, loved tuna. The second is that she didn't like anything else. The third is that giving her tuna— a relatively nutritious food—meant that she at least ate something that was good for her at lunchtime. The fourth is that giving her tuna every day meant that one less time-consuming decision had to be made early in the morning, when the phone rings louder than usual, the clock seems to be moving at double-time and tempers are short. And the fifth: trying to come up with imaginative lunches every day seemed to be a task so difficult that no one in the Gilbar household was willing to undertake it.

But, after the 101st day, none of these reasons was good enough. Something had to be done.

Enter Daddy. Bent on improving his daughter's eating habits, while at the same time making her smile with anticipation when she opened her lunch box, Gary Gilbar began experimenting with new lunches.

He started quietly, without much fanfare, but with a lot of guts. He decided to make yet another tuna sandwich, but this time to cut it into the shape of the capital letter *L*—for Lisa, of course. And, brave man that he is, he cut two slices of cheddar cheese

into several capital *L*'s. He threw in some melon *L*'s, a can of apple juice, a napkin, and then he closed the lid. The deed was done.

At three o'clock that very Wednesday, Annie picked Lisa up at her school. The normally talkative-about-anything-but-what-happened-at-school-today eight-year-old was, this time, eager to share the news.

"Guess what?" Lisa demanded, in a tone quite expectant and somewhat smug.

Annie bit. "What?" she asked, predictably.

"Daddy made me an *L* lunch today. Everything was shaped like the letter *L*. It was so neat!" Lisa exclaimed breathlessly, a wide smile on her little face.

Annie, naturally, was ecstatic! "Did you like it? Was it good?" she asked, hoping she hadn't gone too far.

Lisa answered triumphantly. "Well, everybody—I mean everybody—wanted to trade me for it. They were begging me, Mom!"

Annie's heart sank. She took a deep breath, and asked, slowly, deliberately, her practiced voice controlled, "You—traded—your—lunch?"

Lisa turned to her mom and, with some scorn in her voice, said, "Of course not—I ate the whole thing!"

Annie sighed with relief. It was a beginning.

The next natural step was a ham and cheese sandwich cut with a cookie cutter in the shape of a bunny. From then on, preparing lunches that Lisa actually anticipated eating was a piece of cake.

Meanwhile, across town at the Brokaw's, another negotiating session was taking place. Who wanted peanut butter and jelly on which bread? Would

Andrea compromise and eat salmon salad because there was no tuna in the pantry? Was there time to bake Jenny's favorite zucchini muffins? No more of Tom's granola mix in the cupboard? Couldn't he please make some more for Sarah? The three Brokaw girls, who are all now in college, vividly remember breakfast bargaining sessions, routinely carried out while everyone was in a hurry, the phone was ringing, book bags were misplaced and after-school schedules were yet to be made.

Over at the Chambers's, Veronica can't forget tackling one more plea for something sweet and sugary and less "but it's good for you" food in the lunch box. Chris and Katy had been on an unrelenting campaign to get more sugar and less potassium into their lunch boxes. By that day, Veronica had had enough. Just as she was turning to let out a yelp of frustration at the children's lack of appreciation for the importance of nutrition, a light went on in her head. It was so simple—what a great way to make her point! Why hadn't she thought of it before?

Veronica marched to the pantry, lunch boxes in hand, dug into her leftover Halloween candy bag, and filled the boxes with any sugar-saturated foods she could find (we're talking M&Ms, brownies, chocolate kisses, Snickers, double chocolate cookies, lemon drops, jelly beans and even a Ding Dong). Innocent Chris and Katy grabbed their closed lunch boxes and ran off hurriedly.

That afternoon, it was a worried Veronica who awaited the children's return. Promptly at 3:00 Chris and Katy ran through the front door and yelled, "Mom! Mom! Help! Enough! We need some healthy food—quick!"

At the Gordon home, it was a different story completely. Ronna Gordon is a champion lunch-box packer. But, as it happens to us all, one morning she ran out of absolutely everything—there was truly nothing in the refrigerator or the pantry for Amanda's lunch. After a frantic search, Ronna found some day-old bread (which she promptly toasted), a bit of mustard and two slices of cooked bacon. "No choice," she said to herself. So she made a mustard sandwich, added the bacon on the side, and, hoping for the best, sent Amanda off to school.

When Amanda returned that afternoon, she casually said, "By the way, Mom. Today was our field trip, and when all the mothers saw my lunch, they suggested that maybe I should make my own lunches from now on!"

The stories abound. No doubt, you have more than your share. Whenever we mention lunch boxes to people, eager tales come rushing out. Getting kids to eat, getting a handle on morning bargaining sessions, dealing with kids' wishes versus our own, managing last minute crises—these are all facts of our daily lives. Frustrating, and, at times, disheartening? Of course. But impossible to deal with? Not at all.

Dealing successfully with the lunch-box reality is easier than you imagine. It takes some planning, some creativity, some knowledge of nutrition, some hints on packing, some recipes at hand and a large dose of humor—and you've got it made.

In *The Penny Whistle Lunch Box Book*, we have compiled a simple, commonsense guide that tells you everything you ever wanted and needed to know about planning, cooking and packing a lunch

★

Parker O'Halloran, in first grade, always insisted on the same lunch every day: peanut butter and jelly sandwich, carrot sticks, an apple, two cookies and milk. When mom Susan asked him why, the reply was memorable: "You know, Mom, I never know just what is going to happen at school, so I need to be able to at least count on my lunch!"

★

Jonathan Strauss likes to make his own lunch. Now that he is in third grade, he has progressed from sandwiches to salads. This year's favorite is a cottage cheese invention. Jonathan takes a cup of cottage cheese and puts it in a small mixing bowl. He cuts up tomatoes, scallions, cucumber and radishes (about ¼ cup of each) and mixes them into the cheese. He then sprinkles ½ teaspoon of caraway seeds, a pinch of black pepper and paprika, mixes the salad and puts a portion in his plastic container with its cover.

for your child (and, incidentally, for anyone else). We compared notes with our friends, mothers and fathers at various schools, pediatricians and nutritionists (some of whom are parents themselves). We talked to teachers, to chefs, to anyone who had ever put anything edible in a child's lunch box—or any lunch box.

Thus, on these pages, you will find information on nutrition so your child's lunch will be selected from healthful food groups; ideas for making lunches attractive and interesting; hints on how and when to plan the contents of a lunch box, on how to pack it and how to make it a personal gift to your child; thoughts on including your child in the planning process; plus over 100 recipes to fill your child's lunch box.

And, best of all, you, too, will never again have to make a tuna sandwich on wheat bread, dry, no lettuce or tomato.

A Word About Nutrition

We are not believers in extremes of any kind. We don't think that Jennifer or Jason or Jill will suffer irreparable damage if an occasional hot dog or chocolate cupcake crosses those little lips. Neither do we believe that cereal sprinkled with chocolate sauce or a Twinkie with a side of potato chips constitutes a proper meal. We think tofu may be slightly overrated and the dangers of salt underrated. There is, as they so often say, a "happy medium"—meals that are nutritionally balanced and are also tasty and attractive.

The key is nutrition. If we remind ourselves how little our children's stomachs are, it is easy to understand the importance of the foods we give them. Filling those tummies properly is our responsibility, one that can easily be fulfilled.

Everyone—that means pediatricians, nutritionists, dentists, teachers and even the government of the United States (or at least the U.S. Department of Agriculture [USDA] and the National Academy of Sciences' National Research Council, Food and Nutrition Board)—recommends that a child eat a certain number of servings from four food groups every day. They are milk and dairy products, meats, fruits and vegetables, and cereals. USDA guidelines suggest that a child of any age (with teenagers needing a little more than four- to ten-year-olds) should consume, daily:

three portions of milk products
(three glasses of milk and/or yogurt, cottage cheese or any sliced cheese);

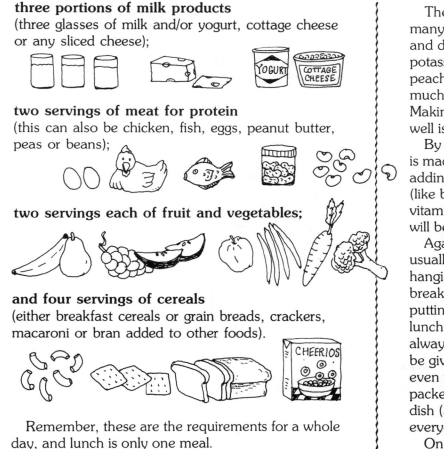

two servings of meat for protein
(this can also be chicken, fish, eggs, peanut butter, peas or beans);

two servings each of fruit and vegetables;

and four servings of cereals
(either breakfast cereals or grain breads, crackers, macaroni or bran added to other foods).

Remember, these are the requirements for a whole day, and lunch is only one meal.

You can, if you like, get more specific about the nutritional requirements recommended for children. For example, USDA guidelines recommend that kids four to eight years old consume between 1,800 and 2,400 calories a day; that they need 30 to 36 grams of protein, 800 milligrams of calcium, 2,000 units of vitamin A, 15 milligrams of iron, and so on.

These are the government's suggestions. But, how many parents—even the most conscientious moms and dads—measure how many milligrams of potassium and phosphorus are in the cup of canned peaches in syrup our kids eat? It's asking too much—and, more important, it is unnecessary. Making sure our kids—and all of us lunchers—eat well is actually quite simple.

By insuring that, as often as possible, each meal is made up of the four groups of food, and by adding certain highly healthy foods to all our meals (like broccoli and parsley, which are very high in vitamin A, calcium and potassium), chances are we will be eating properly.

Again, remember that lunch is only one meal—usually the only one your child will eat without you hanging around. So our suggestion is—make sure breakfast and dinner are highly nutritious. Then, by putting together a nourishing, attractive and tasty lunch-box menu, together with your children (so they always have at least one very favorite choice), you'll be giving them the best meal possible. And then, even if they eat only two of the three items you packed and trade the third for a not-so-nutritious dish (and they *will* trade, we guarantee you), everyone concerned is still ahead of the game.

On page 88, you will find a chart of most of the foods contained in the Penny Whistle recipes and their nutritional contents. Read this list carefully—don't try to memorize it. Just digest it to find out some interesting facts about the foods you know and love. Once you know what the foods contain, go about the business of planning and making the recipes we've included. *You don't have to measure*

★
Whenever you give a dinner party and you have leftovers, think of the kids' lunch the next day. Creamy french cheeses, pâté, stuffed mushrooms, celery sticks, sliced meat—all make great surprise treats to a kid who is used to peanut butter.

★

In a pinch, Ronna Gordon puts a frozen burrito (with beans and cheese) in the microwave in the morning, then wraps it in foil and puts it in the lunch box. Josh and Gabe Gordon are always happy with this alternative.

VEGETABLES

and count the calcium and protein. We've done it for you. And the recipes are, in most cases (desserts have to be an exception), made up of healthful foods that, when put together in the lunch box, will constitute a well-planned nutritional lunch.

By creating your own menus with the Penny Whistle Lunch Box recipes, you will automatically be including foods from each food group. By choosing one dish from various sections (one meat sandwich, a fruit dish, a cheese or milk choice and a drink) you will easily create the best lunch box for your child.

Here's an example. Marc Gilbar is eight years old. Nutritionists and the United States government believe he should have at least 3,500 units of

vitamin A, 35 grams of protein and 900 milligrams of calcium each and every day.

Sounds intimidating? Not if you choose one dish from the various food groups. Not if you know that packing his lunch box with a tuna salad on wheat bread sandwich (made with tuna, hard-cooked egg, and a tablespoon of chopped parsley and some minced broccoli) gives him an immediate fix of 590 units of vitamin A, 30 grams of protein and 41 milligrams of calcium. When we add four dates stuffed with cream cheese, Marc gets an additional 4,400 units of vitamin A and 40 milligrams of calcium. Add a corn muffin (another 100 units of vitamin A, 90 milligrams of calcium and 3 grams of protein)—and we've got it made! Marc has eaten a

MEATS/POULTRY

FISH

BREADS/MUFFINS

FRUITS

PEANUTS/PEANUT BUTTER

SOUPS

TREATS/SNACKS

CHEESE/MILK/EGGS

delicious *and* nutritious lunch, even given the possibility that he traded a couple of dates for a bag of tortilla chips.

Again, our advice is to familiarize yourself with the nutritional information to make yourself more knowledgeable. It will also help you understand why the Penny Whistle recipes contain certain foods— why we like pumpkin bread (it is chock full of vitamin A and potassium), why broccoli and parsley are valuable extra added attractions in any salad (calcium), and why we add peanuts to salads and desserts (protein). You will also learn why certain foods, when combined with others, give your child a totally healthful meal, and why others are not so great together (perhaps they offer too much sodium at one time or too many calories, at the expense of other more healthful ingredients).

The beauty of all this organization is that all the nutritional research has been done for you—you won't ever need to have a calculator on hand to figure out what your child will eat today. The Penny Whistle recipes take all this information into account, so when you pack your child's lunch box in the morning, you can be sure it contains a healthful meal.

We have marked those recipes that require some advance preparation. This will make it easier for you to plan menus at the beginning of the week. For example, if you roast chicken on Sunday night, you know you will be able to make variations on that theme for most of the week. If you've made peanut butter bread, your child will know what treats lie ahead.

Involving Your Child

The idea of involving your child in decisions that affect his or her life is not a new one, but it is one which we strongly believe in. In our first book, *The Penny Whistle Party Planner,* we stressed the importance of sharing the decision-making process of planning his or her birthday party with your child. The same is true, to some extent, in planning your child's lunch. Now, we are not here to say that you should hand over control to your child—whatever he wants, he gets. On the contrary, giving children such authority and power is not healthy and most often results in an unmanageable environment. Rather, we suggest you include your child in the process of planning, which will result in having a child who feels important (because you have considered his opinion), who feels involved in what goes on in his life (because you let him have a say in it), and who will be more likely to eat the lunch you and he have planned together.

Participation in the process is important and easy. Encourage your child to look through the book and choose lunch-box menus with you. Some democracy in the kitchen can help make your child more interested in what will appear in the lunch box. Choices, not challenges, make for a happier child who will then be more inclined to eat what you give him. You can put your child in charge of choosing the lunch menus for the week by making a Lunch Box Calendar and noting his choice for each day.

★

Leslie Alexandra Cohen may be only three, but she insists on making her lunch for nursery school. She spreads her own peanut butter topped with jelly. Leslie didn't care if the sandwiches looked a little sloppy and slightly misshapen. Neither did her mother, Jean, who thought it was more important that Leslie have the confidence to make her own lunch than to have the sandwiches look perfect. The next step? Jean is teaching Leslie how to cut the sandwiches with her cookie cutters.

Veronica Chambers tells her favorite lunch box story: "After making the kids' lunches yet another night, I got this bright idea to take a huge bite out of their sandwiches and granola bars and stick a note inside saying, 'Kilroy was here!' When the kids returned home that afternoon, neither one said a word. But that night at dinner, Katy and Chris insisted on my letting them serve me dinner. Imagine my surprise when they gave me an empty plate with a note saying: 'Kilroy was here, too!'

Want to add zip to a cream cheese sandwich? Janice Payne's son Juston swears by a dash of jalapeño jelly on cream cheese on whole wheat bread.

A four-year-old can check off the lunch as it's eaten and then put a sticker on the menu he liked. An older child can develop a system with the calendar to keep track of which lunches are favorites, which desserts he or she prefers with which main dish and so on.

It's really a simple process. Together, at the beginning of the week (and not in the morning, when everyone has more than his share of decisions to make and tasks to accomplish), sit with your child and plan the week's menus. Using our method of choosing dishes from different food groups for each day's lunch, make those choices according to what you have in the house, what your child likes and what you have the time and inclination to prepare. Then, for every day's menu, leave a black space for your child to fill in. Thus, one day, your child can fill in his choice of dessert, and another day he gets to choose from the cheese category, and another from the meat recipes.

And if your child is at all interested, cook together. Even very young children get a kick out of helping in the smallest of ways—holding a pan, breaking an egg or keeping track of the cookie cutters. And older children will enjoy making some of the lunches independently—they are designed to be both simple and fun.

You can also shop together. Take the Perfect Pantry list (see page 85), add to it the ingredients in the recipes your kids want to make and go to the market together. Let your kids use their creativity so they feel they've had input into what they eat. If you have made them Crunchy Chicken Salad and they see a special on pink salmon and want to try it with this recipe—do it. Or, if they see a cookie cutter in a funny shape, buy it if you can. A 69-cent cookie cutter is worth a fortune if it can create a new and enticing sandwich for your child. We believe you will find that spending this time together is very rewarding, both personally and nutritionally.

Planning & Preparing Lunch

It's 8:00 A.M. Your watch refuses to slow down and the phone insists on ringing yet again. Your child is at the breakfast table, half dressed, eyelids still drooping, munching on toast and moving the eggs on the plate. Is this the time to ask, "What do *you* want that's special for lunch?"

★

*Things to fill with salads,
meatballs or sliced cheese
and meat:*
  wontons
  pitas
  empanadas
  tortillas
  apples
  lettuce leaves
  crescent rolls
  snow peas
  baked potato skins

No! It's too late for negotiations, too late to instantly come up with a lunch that is interesting and nutritious, too late to go to the market to get those items your recipes require and you forgot. It's not a great time for dictatorial messages either— "You'll have the tuna and you'll like it!"

Breakfast should not be a battleground for lunch. Rather, breakfast should be a pleasant beginning to your child's day. Therefore, planning lunch should be done either at other times or at least in other ways.

There are two alternatives to this daily battle of choices. One is to plan the lunches on Sunday (or any "night before") and even to make some of the recipes at that time. This will result in your knowing the week's menus ahead of time. (In the index you will find a list of recipes that should be prepared ahead of time.) Sunday night cooking can be a lot of fun. Moreover, the more organized you are before morning time, the freer you'll be each A.M. Almost every Sunday night we broil or roast one chicken, so that we can make different chicken dishes during the first half of the week.

The other alternative to the Sunday lunch brigade is to make the many other recipes every morning. These are simple, fast and fun. And having the perfect pantry full of all the different items you'll need gives you the flexibility to make any of these lunches almost at the drop of a hat.

The Creative Lunch Box

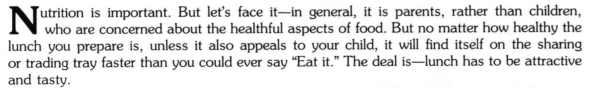

Nutrition is important. But let's face it—in general, it is parents, rather than children, who are concerned about the healthful aspects of food. But no matter how healthy the lunch you prepare is, unless it also appeals to your child, it will find itself on the sharing or trading tray faster than you could ever say "Eat it." The deal is—lunch has to be attractive and tasty.

Tasty is easy because all of these recipes have been developed to be delicious. After all, what's the use of giving a child something that is good for him if it tastes awful or is boring and plain? Our recipes also take into account the fact that children like a variety of flavors. For example,

Sometimes Joyce Bogart has to be out of town in the middle of the week. To ensure Evan, Jenna and Taylor are not lonely, she makes sure they can "hear" from her even though she's miles away. Joyce prepares a series of little notes and gives them to the kids' babysitter to put into each lunch box. Sometimes she mentions specific things ("Remember, soccer practice is today"; "Have fun in rocketry class"; "Good luck on your spelling test—I know you'll do great!"), and other times she just sends love notes to remind the kids that she is thinking of them even though she is not there.

the combination of bacon and dates is so good because the contrast of sweet and savory is pleasing to the palate. And many of the recipes call for ingredients that are high in natural sugars, satisfying children's desire for sweets. Others have some salt in them—just enough to satisfy that craving for the salty taste of food. (But, in general, we believe it is wise to try to limit any foods that are high in sodium. This does not mean you must never again give your child a piece of salami—but giving it to him *every* day of the week is another story.)

And then there is the look of lunch. We as adults are always concerned with the food we present to guests when we entertain. But let's not forget that children love pretty things! They delight in unusual shapes and in clever design, especially when it is unexpected and when it will be unveiled in front of an audience of their friends. The first time Gary gave Lisa her ham and cheese bunnies, she was the hit of her class—so proud to be the only child in school who had bunnies for lunch, and equally excited about eating her prize.

Making foods cleverly attractive is easier than you think—just read through the recipes and see how nearly all of them are, in one way or another, pretty and thereby enticing. And it is so easy to do! A set of cookie cutters in the shapes of toys or animals can make a sandwich or other food an extra-delightful treat. Forming foods in different and unusual shapes is another trick. Rolling ham, making a lollipop out of turkey and a bread stick, or filling little dates with cream cheese are all simple ways to make foods appealing to your child's eye.

Another important consideration in creating a lunch box your child will love is making it a *personal* lunch for him. This does not refer to the choice of food—you've already done that when you and your child chose the lunch-box menus together. "Personal" means doing something for your child that will make him smile or remind him of you when he is away from home. Including something of yourself in the lunch box is shared intimacy when apart, a way to say "I love you!", "Good luck with your test!", etc.

Some suggestions:

◆◆◆ On Sunday night when you are preparing the basics for some of your lunches for the week, make a batch of fortune cookies (see page 72 for the recipe). Write out some personal messages that your child will appreciate—a funny joke, a reminder of how much he or she is loved, a surprise preview of upcoming events—anything that will make your child smile.

◆◆◆ Get a stack of stickers in all shapes and sizes. If your child carries a lunch bag, put the stickers on the outside. If she carries a lunch box, put the stickers on any wrapping inside.

◆◆◆ You can write a personal message on an attractive label and fasten it to a wrapped sandwich.

◆◆◆ Write your child a note—not a reminder to clean her room when she gets home, but a love note or funny message. It will mean a lot and will put her in a good mood so she will be more likely to eat and enjoy her lunch.

◆◆◆ If you planned the menu with your child, throw in an extra treat that will be a pleasant surprise with a note saying "Surprise! Mom sent me!"

◆◆◆ If your child uses paper bags for her lunch, try buying interesting ones. They come in colors and with designs such as gingham and polka dots.

◆◆◆ Order a rubber stamp with your child's name on it. All children, from those who are just starting to read to the more sophisticated twelve-year-olds, love to see their names in print. Stamp anything you can with your child's name—the paper lunch sack, the napkin inside, the label you include or a piece of stationery.

◆◆◆ All the kids we know love jokes and riddles—the sillier, the better. If your child is like any of ours and has a favorite joke book, choose some he loves and copy them on a card. Include the card in the lunch box. You can probably imagine the smile on your child's face when his favorite joke appears in his lunch.

◆◆◆ Start a cookie cutter collection—it is an inexpensive and simple way to make lunches delightful. Any sandwich when cut into a funny shape will amuse your child—and will induce him to eat his lunch. Besides, it is fun looking for different shapes whenever you shop with your child.

◆◆◆ Magic markers—especially the extra-thick ones—are terrific for writing your child's name or for drawing on the outside of the lunch bag (or even for making faces on hard-cooked egg shells or bananas).

◆◆◆ If your child likes to trade at lunchtime, be sure to include a food treat that is "valuable" in his or her mind—an extra fruit leather or a bag of peanuts or freshly made popcorn are special favorites among the trading set.

★

When Armen Weitzman was four, there were times when he didn't want to eat what those around him were having for lunch. Maggie's rule was to always have a fruit plate packed. Armen soon learned that he couldn't just choose whatever he wanted—if he didn't want what he was given, he could always have his fruit plate.

★

When Barbara Maller's children, Kerry and Heidi, decided to give up lunch boxes for lunch bags, Barbara bought rubber stamps with their names on them and stamped each bag in the morning. That way, Heidi's famous baked-by-hand chocolate chip cookies never got mixed up with Kerry's granola munchies.

Packing the Lunch Box

Packing a lunch that won't spoil means making a concentrated effort to cook foods properly, to wrap them carefully and to use only foods you know are fresh. Linda Brown, director of food and nutrition at Childrens Hospital Los Angeles, explains, "The things you want to watch out for in terms of spoilage problems are protein foods. Meat should be fresh and cold when put into the lunch box. Mayonnaise, that old worry, is really generally safe, especially if it has just been taken out of the refrigerator. What you are really concerned with is the egg and milk components of the food." Often this worry is unfounded because room temperatures are pretty constant, and unless your child eats his lunch in the desert, chances are the

mayonnaise, for instance, will not spoil. But it is important to keep mayonnaise in the refrigerator once you have opened the jar and to make sure you keep all salads and sandwich fillings refrigerated. Then, if you pack the lunch at 8:30 in the morning, it easily should stay fresh until noon.

For keeping foods hot, the good old thermos is still your best bet. Certain foods—hot dogs or ham kabobs, for example—can be warmed in the oven in the morning and wrapped in aluminum foil to keep the heat until lunchtime.

Here are some more hints on storing foods properly from the U.S. Department of Agriculture and from Linda Brown:

♦♦♦ Make sure you always cook food thoroughly.

♦♦♦ Work with clean hands, both when cooking and packing. Remember, fingers spread bacteria.

♦♦♦ In warm weather, freeze your bread. In the morning, take out the number of slices you need, spread with your choice of filling and then wrap. The bread will work as an insulator and will thaw out by lunchtime.

♦♦♦ You can freeze small cans of juice and pack them in the lunch box. The can will keep everything else in the lunch box cool and will itself thaw out so your child can then drink the juice. If your child carries lunch in a bag, put the can into a plastic bag first, otherwise it will sweat as it thaws and will destroy the bag.

♦♦♦ In a hot climate, enclose a "blue ice" in the lunch box. They can be bought in any supermarket or hardware store and come in lunch-box sizes.

♦♦♦ In warm weather you may also want to use an insulated lunch box rather than a paper bag. They are much more efficient for keeping food cool.

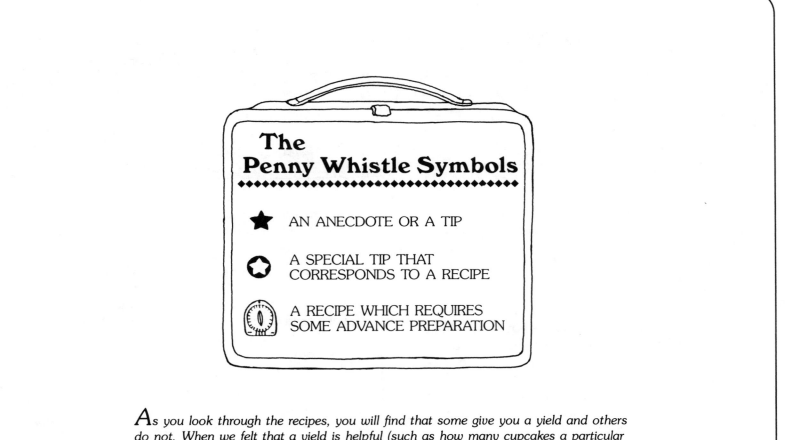

As you look through the recipes, you will find that some give you a yield and others do not. When we felt that a yield is helpful (such as how many cupcakes a particular recipe will make) we have included it. But often the yield depends on the age of your child and/or the amount he or she (or even yourself) will eat. Thus, when we make our salmon salad sandwiches, the yield depends on how many slices your child will eat, and how thick or thin he likes the salmon spread. As we moms and dads already know, whatever is left can be refrigerated and kept for the day after.

Recipes

BREADS/MUFFINS

APPLESAUCE AND NUT BREAD
CORN MUFFIN SURPRISE
BLUEBERRY MUFFINS
BANANA BREAD
IN-A-HURRY CHEESE STICKS
CRANBERRY BREAD
CARROT CAKE
DILL BREAD
SESAME CHEESE STICKS
PENNY WHISTLE PIZZA DOUGH
RYE MELBA TOAST
ALL-SEASON PUMPKIN BREAD
SPANISH CORN BREAD

Applesauce and Nut Bread

1¾ cups sifted all-purpose flour
2 teaspoons baking powder
½ cup sugar
¾ teaspoon salt
½ teaspoon ground cinnamon
½ teaspoon ground nutmeg
1 cup granola
½ cup chopped nuts
⅓ cup raisins
2 tablespoons wheat germ
1½ cups unsweetened applesauce
1 egg
3 tablespoons vegetable oil

Preheat the oven to 300 degrees. Butter two 9- x 5-inch loaf pans or one loaf pan and one 12-cup muffin tin.

In a bowl, sift together the flour, baking powder, sugar, salt, cinnamon and nutmeg. Stir in the granola, nuts, raisins and wheat germ. Set the mixture aside.

In another bowl, mix together the applesauce, egg and oil. Add to the flour mixture and stir until well combined.

Divide the batter among the prepared baking pans. Bake for about 1 hour (about 35 minutes for muffins), or until a toothpick inserted in the center comes out clean. The bread may require up to 10 minutes more baking time.

Cool the bread in the pan on a wire rack for 30 minutes. Turn out on the rack and let cool completely. Wrap well and store in the refrigerator or on the counter.

When your are making lunch, slice the bread and spread with cream cheese (making an open sandwich). Cover with plastic wrap. This nutritious bread is absolutely delicious by itself, too.

Corn Muffin Surprise

1 cup cornmeal
1 cup all-purpose flour
1 teaspoon baking soda
1 cup shredded cheddar cheese
⅓ cup (5⅓ tablespoons) butter or margarine, at room temperature
½ cup buttermilk or milk
2 eggs, beaten
1 tablespoon sugar (optional)
Jam (any flavor your child likes)

Preheat the oven to 350 degrees. Butter a 12-cup muffin tin.

In a mixing bowl, blend together all of the ingredients except the jam.

Half-fill each muffin cup with batter. Add ½ teaspoon jam to each muffin. Add more batter until each cup is three-quarters full.

Bake for 30 minutes, or until a toothpick inserted in the center comes out clean. Cool on a wire rack.

★

Favorite fillings for Pita Pockets:
- *sliced turkey with shredded cheddar cheese, slices of red or green pepper and a teaspoon of chutney*
- *sliced avocado, crumbled bacon, shredded mozzarella cheese and a dab of sour cream*
- *falafel balls, hummus, chopped tomatoes, shredded lettuce and slices of pickles*
- *cream cheese, slices of roast beef, chopped scallions and chopped tomatoes*
- *chopped pineapple, slivers of ham or smoked turkey and honey mustard*
- *egg salad, lettuce and relish*
- *tuna salad with marinated artichoke hearts*
- *slices of ham and cheddar cheese, melted in the toaster oven*

✪

This is Aunt Ida Anolik's muffin recipe that she has been making for her nieces and nephews for many years. If she is out of blueberries, she has substituted other berries or raisins. The outcome is always delicious!

★

Barbara Bosson Bochco makes blueberry muffins that everybody fights for. Her secret is sprinkling the tops with cinnamon and sugar.

Blueberry Muffins

¾ cup milk
½ cup safflower oil
1 egg
1 teaspoon vanilla extract
2 cups all-purpose flour
½ cup sugar
1 tablespoon baking powder
Pinch of salt
½ cup fresh or frozen blueberries, mashed
1 cup fresh or frozen blueberries
(thawed and drained if frozen)

Preheat the oven to 400 degrees. Fit a 12-cup muffin tin with paper liners.

In a mixing bowl, blend together the milk, oil, egg and vanilla. Add the flour, sugar, baking powder and salt and mix by hand with a wooden spoon until moistened. (The batter will be lumpy.)

Add the mashed blueberries and mix well (this will give the batter a bluish-purplish color). Carefully mix in the whole blueberries, taking care not to break them.

Spoon the batter into the muffin liners, filling them about three-quarters full. Bake for 20 minutes, or until a toothpick inserted in the center comes out clean. Cool on a wire rack.

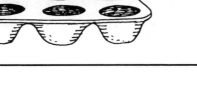

Banana Bread

½ cup (1 stick) butter or margarine, at room temperature
¾ cup packed brown sugar
1 egg
1 cup whole wheat flour
½ cup unbleached white flour
1 teaspoon baking soda
½ teaspoon salt (optional)
¼ teaspoon ground cinnamon (optional)
2 or 3 ripe bananas, mashed
¼ cup buttermilk or plain yogurt
1 cup chopped walnuts or sunflower seeds
(optional)

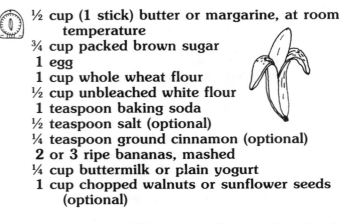

Preheat the oven to 350 degrees. Butter a 9- x 5-inch loaf pan.

In the bowl of an electric mixer, cream the butter with the sugar until the mixture is fluffy and light brown in color. Beat in the egg.

On a sheet of waxed paper, sift together the flours, baking soda, salt and cinnamon.

In a small bowl, combine the bananas and buttermilk and stir until well blended.

Alternately add the flour mixture and banana mixture to the creamed butter, mixing thoroughly after each addition, and beating until all of the ingredients are thoroughly combined. Fold in the walnuts by hand.

Pour the batter into the prepared loaf pan and smooth the top. Bake for 50 minutes to 1 hour, or until a toothpick inserted in the center of the loaf comes out clean.

Let the bread stand in the pan on a wire rack for at least 15 minutes. Remove from the pan and let sit at room temperature, uncovered, for at least 1 hour. (If you try to cut this bread when it is warm, it will crumble.) When firm, wrap in plastic wrap.

In the morning, decide if you want the bread to be a lunchtime dessert or a main course. If you decide on dessert, cut a 1-inch-thick slice and wrap. If you want it to be the main course, cut thin slices and spread with cheese, peanut butter or jam, and close as a sandwich.

In-A-Hurry Cheese Sticks

3 slices sourdough bread, crusts removed
Butter or margarine, at room temperature
½ cup grated cheddar cheese

Spread the bread slices with butter. Sprinkle on the cheese. Chill, covered, in the refrigerator overnight. (If you make this in the morning, allow time for chilling.)

Cut each bread slice into 1-inch-wide strips. Toast both sides in a toaster oven or broiler until browned, 5 to 10 minutes. Wrap in foil.

MAKES 9 STICKS

Cranberry Bread

2 cups sifted all-purpose flour
½ teaspoon salt
1½ teaspoons baking powder
½ teaspoon baking soda
1 cup sugar
1 egg, lightly beaten
2 tablespoons safflower oil
¾ cup fresh orange juice
1 cup cranberry sauce
½ cup whole cranberries
½ cup chopped nuts
Grated zest of 1 orange

Preheat the oven to 350 degrees. Butter and flour a 9- x 5-inch loaf pan.

In a mixing bowl, sift together the dry ingredients. Add the egg, oil and orange juice. Mix with a fork or spoon until moistened. Gently stir in the cranberry sauce, cranberries, nuts and orange zest, taking care not to mash the cranberries.

Pour the mixture into the prepared loaf pan. Bake for 45 minutes, or until a toothpick inserted in the center comes out clean. Cool, uncovered, for 30 minutes. Store wrapped in plastic wrap in a bread box or in the refrigerator.

★
Melissa Epp came up with a great use for stale bread. She takes day-old slices and lets them dry in the air for 2 to 3 days, then puts them in an oven at 250 degrees for 15 to 20 minutes. The result is perfect homemade melba toast for lunch.

✪
If your children like poppy or sesame seeds, add them to the cheese and sprinkle together. It's a nice change from plain cheese sticks.

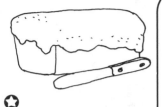

This Carrot Cake is a great bread. But if you want to pack it as a dessert, use this frosting.

Carrot Cake

1 cup packed brown sugar
1 cup granulated sugar
4 cups grated carrots
½ cup raisins
1⅓ cups pineapple juice
1½ teaspoons ground cinnamon
1 teaspoon ground allspice
½ teaspoon ground nutmeg
¼ teaspoon ground cloves
Dash of ground ginger
3 eggs, beaten
2 tablespoons safflower oil
1 cup crushed pineapple, with 1⅓ cups juice reserved
2½ cups stirred all-purpose flour
2 teaspoons baking soda
1½ teaspoons baking powder
1 teaspoon salt
¾ cup coarsely chopped walnuts

Preheat the oven to 350 degrees. Butter a large loaf pan (about 11 x 6 inches).

In a saucepan, over low heat, combine the sugars, carrots, raisins, pineapple juice and all of the spices. Simmer, stirring occasionally, for 10 minutes. Set aside to cool to room temperature.

Mix in the eggs and oil.

Place the crushed pineapple in a sieve set over a bowl. Drain and reserve the juice. Add the drained pineapple to the carrot mixture.

In a bowl, combine the flour, baking soda, baking powder, salt and walnuts; mix well. Add to the carrot mixture and stir to mix thoroughly.

Spread the batter into the prepared loaf pan. Bake for 45 minutes, or until a toothpick inserted in the center comes out clean. Cool in the pan on a rack. Remove from the pan and frost with Cream Cheese Frosting.

CREAM CHEESE FROSTING

4 ounces cream cheese (½ large package), at room temperature
2 tablespoons butter, at room temperature
1 cup powdered sugar
1 tablespoon fresh lemon juice

In the bowl of an electric mixer, cream together the cream cheese and butter. Beat in the sugar and lemon juice. Spread on the Carrot Cake.

Dill Bread

Michael Roberts, the chef at Trump's restaurant in Beverly Hills, California, is a master at clever and delicious combinations of foods. Here is a favorite:

2½ cups all-purpose flour
¼ cup sugar
3½ teaspoons baking powder
1 bunch fresh dill, chopped
    Finely grated zest of 1 orange
1¼ cups buttermilk
3 tablespoons vegetable oil
1 egg

Preheat the oven to 350 degrees. Butter and flour 1 large loaf pan (about 11 x 6 inches) or 2 smaller pans.

Combine the flour, sugar, baking powder, dill and orange zest in a blender or food processor. Mix well. Add the buttermilk, oil and egg. Mix until smooth.

Pour the batter into the prepared pan. Bake for about 25 minutes, or until a toothpick inserted in the center comes out clean. Cool on a wire rack. Wrap in plastic wrap.

In the morning, slice the loaf into sandwich slices. It is great with smoked salmon or salmon salad. Other variations include these:

Substitute 1 bunch of fresh sage for the dill and serve slices of ham and Swiss cheese on the bread.
Substitute 1 bunch of oregano for the dill and serve sliced tomatoes and cheese on the sandwich.

Substitute 1 cup diced bananas for the dill and use peanut butter and jelly as a sandwich spread.

The bread will keep well for 5 to 7 days in the refrigerator. You can also freeze it.

Sesame Cheese Sticks

1 cup all-purpose flour
½ teaspoon salt
⅛ teaspoon cayenne pepper
½ cup (1 stick) butter, cut into bits and at room temperature
½ cup finely grated sharp cheddar cheese
1 to 2 tablespoons milk
¼ cup sesame seeds

Preheat the oven to 400 degrees.

In a bowl, sift together the flour, salt and cayenne pepper. Blend in the butter until the mixture resembles coarse meal. Add the cheese and mix well. Gradually add enough of the milk to make a sticky dough.

On a lightly floured surface, roll out the dough ¾ inch thick. Sprinkle on the sesame seeds and press them lightly into the dough. Cut the dough into ½-inch-wide strips, 2 inches long.

Place the strips of dough on an ungreased baking sheet. Bake for 8 to 10 minutes, or until crisp and golden brown. Cool on a wire rack and store in a covered tin.

MAKES 8 TO 10 STICKS

✪
Spread the Cheese Sticks with butter or margarine and roll sliced meat around them.

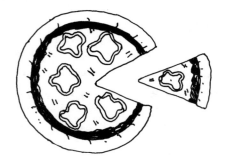

Penny Whistle Pizza Dough

3 tablespoons lukewarm water
3 tablespoons milk
1¼ teaspoons (about ½ package) active
    dried yeast
Pinch of sugar
1 tablespoon olive oil
¼ teaspoon salt
1 tablespoon rye flour
2 tablespoons whole wheat flour
½ cup plus 2 tablespoons unbleached
    white flour
Pizza toppings of your choice

In a small bowl, combine the lukewarm water and milk (the temperature should not be much warmer than body temperature or it will kill the yeast). Add the yeast and sugar, stirring to dissolve the yeast. Set aside for 10 minutes.

Meanwhile, in a large bowl, combine the olive oil, salt, rye flour and whole wheat flour. When the yeast is foamy, add it to the large bowl and mix well. Gradually add the white flour, stirring until it forms a soft, workable dough. Add only enough flour to keep the dough from sticking (it should be a little moist). Turn the dough onto a lightly floured surface and knead for about 5 minutes.

Lightly oil a clean bowl. Place the dough in the bowl and turn once to coat with oil. Cover and let rise in a warm draft-free place until doubled in bulk, 35 to 40 minutes.

Preheat the oven to 500 degrees. Flour a 12-inch pizza pan.

Punch down the dough and shape it into a ball. Roll out on a floured surface, stretching the dough with your hands into a 10-inch circle, leaving it slightly thicker around the edges.

Place the dough on the pizza pan and cover with the toppings of your choice.

Bake for 20 minutes, or until the crust is lightly browned.

Rye Melba Toast

Thin-sliced rye bread
Butter

Preheat the oven to 250 degrees.

Butter one side of each slice of bread. Place the bread, buttered side up, on a baking sheet. Bake until dried out and lightly browned, about 8 to 10 minutes.

✪ *You can use all white flour in the Pizza Dough instead of whole wheat and rye flour. Ingredients for the topping can be prepared while the dough is rising.*

✪ *Make the Pizza Dough the day before and refrigerate, covered. You can bake the pizza in the morning.*

✪ *For seasoned Melba Toast, simply sprinkle with garlic powder, dill or other spices before baking.*

All-Season Pumpkin Bread

2 cups self-rising flour
1 cup sugar
1 cup canned pumpkin puree
3 eggs
⅓ cup vegetable oil
2 teaspoons ground cinnamon
½ teaspoon ground cloves
Pinch of ground nutmeg
½ cup raisins

Preheat the oven to 350 degrees. Butter a 9- x 5-inch loaf pan.

In a large bowl, combine all of the ingredients, stirring with a wooden spoon until well mixed.

Pour the batter into the prepared pan. Bake for 40 to 50 minutes, or until a toothpick inserted in the center comes out clean.

Cool the bread on a rack before removing from the pan. Wrap in a plastic bag and store at room temperature or in the refrigerator.

When you are ready to make lunch, cut off as many slices as your child will eat. If you are serving a plain slice, cut a piece about 1 inch thick and wrap. It is very good plain, even better spread with cream cheese or jam. Cut thinner slices if you are making a sandwich.

Spanish Corn Bread

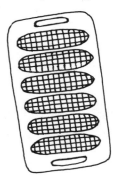

1 cup yellow cornmeal
1 cup all-purpose flour
1 tablespoon baking powder
½ teaspoon salt
2 tablespoons honey
1 egg, lightly beaten
1 cup milk
1 cup fresh or frozen corn kernels
¼ cup olive oil
1 can (4 ounces) peeled whole green chiles, drained, patted dry and coarsely chopped
1 cup grated sharp cheddar cheese (about 6 ounces)

Preheat the oven to 400 degrees. Butter a 9-inch square baking pan.

In a large bowl, sift together the cornmeal, flour, baking powder and salt.

In another bowl, combine the honey, egg, milk, corn kernels and oil. Blend well. Add to the dry ingredients and stir gently until just mixed.

Spread half of the batter into the prepared pan. Sprinkle on the chiles. Cover the chiles with the cheese. Spoon the remaining batter over the cheese.

Place on the bottom rack of the oven. Bake for 35 minutes, or until golden brown. To serve, cut into squares and serve while still warm.

Pour the Corn Bread batter into a cornstick pan for "corn-shaped" muffins.

This Pumpkin Bread is the simplest bread we make. It takes so little preparation and time and is wonderful to make on Sunday night. It will taste delicious throughout the week and can be served in a variety of ways. Annie has often baked two—she uses one for a variety of lunches during the week, and the other she sends to school for the teachers to share with the class. It is always a hit!

This Pumpkin Bread is the most nutritious bread you can eat—full of potassium and vitamin A.

CHEESE/MILK/EGGS

CHEESE AND FRUITWICH
CURRIED EGG CLOVERS
MOM'S TINY EGG BOWLS
MELTED CHEESE SPECIAL
HERB CHEESE SPREAD
SIMPLE CHEESE PIZZAS
YOGURT PANCAKES
PROVOLONE CRISPS

Cheese and Fruitwich

½ cup cream cheese, at room temperature
⅛ cup chopped unsalted peanuts
½ apple, cored, peeled and sliced
    Few drops of fresh lemon juice
2 slices date-nut bread

Combine the cream cheese and nuts in a bowl.

Sprinkle the apple slices with the lemon juice to keep them from turning brown.

Take a slice of date-nut bread, spread with the cheese and nut mixture and cover with apple slices. Use another slice of date-nut bread to top the sandwich and wrap well.

Curried Egg Clovers

¼ cup chopped cooked broccoli
3 hard-cooked eggs, chopped
2 tablespoons chopped onion
¼ teaspoon curry powder (or to taste, optional)
1 tablespoon chopped parsley
2 to 3 tablespoons mayonnaise
2 slices whole wheat bread

In a bowl, combine the broccoli, eggs, onion, curry powder and parsley. Add just enough mayonnaise to bind the ingredients together. Season with salt and pepper to taste.

Cut the crusts off the bread and flatten each slice with a rolling pin. Spread a thin layer of the curried egg salad on the bread and cover with another slice of flattened bread. Cut the sandwich with a clover-shaped cookie cutter. Wrap the sandwich in foil or plastic. Cover the remainder of the spread and keep refrigerated.

MAKES ENOUGH SPREAD FOR 4 SANDWICHES

Mom's Tiny Egg Bowls

2 hard-cooked eggs, peeled, top cut off and yolk scooped out (gently)
Dab of filling

Choose your child's favorite fillings, such as tuna fish salad (the simplest—remember, eggs are small, and you don't have room for a chunky salad), salmon cream filling, cream cheese or chopped liver. Mix the yolk into the filling (your child will never know). Fill the egg-white bowl with a teaspoon of filling and wrap individually in foil or plastic.

✪

Egg Clovers are a very nutritious lunch—the egg, parsley and broccoli provide much-needed vitamin A and potassium.

★

As a child, Annie would eat no eggs—categorically, no eggs. She didn't care about the high content of vitamin A, or about the iron or the calcium or the phosphorus. But Annie's mother, smart as she is, knew how to get around her. She used to make hard-cooked egg bowls and fill them with anything Annie loved. Thus, she got an actual, honest-to-God egg into her little body.

✪

Buy an assortment of cheeses—cheddar, jack or more exotic kinds if your child likes them (gorgonzola, blue cheese, goat cheese) and make a combination grilled cheese sandwich. And don't forget old favorites—grilled bacon and/or pickles—will wake up any grilled sandwich.

✪

Ask your child for his ideas on pizza toppings and combine different ones: use two or more types of cheese for cheese pizza, put them on an English muffin and toast in the oven.

★

This is a variation on the pizza: Georgina Rothenberg has made pita pizza for all three of her now college-age sons. She slices a pita open, toasts it, spreads it with Ragu sauce, tops it with different toppings (pepperoni, mushrooms, olives) and finishes with shredded mozzarella. She places the whole pita in the toaster oven until the cheese melts. It goes off to school wrapped in aluminum foil.

Melted Cheese Special

    1 teaspoon Sweet Mustard (recipe follows)
    2 slices Muenster cheese
    2 slices sourdough or other bread

Spread the mustard on 1 slice of bread. Cover with the cheese and top with the remaining slice of bread. Put the sandwich in the toaster oven and toast until the cheese melts. Wrap in aluminum foil.

SWEET MUSTARD

    1 cup Coleman's dry mustard
    1 cup cider vinegar
    1 cup sugar
    3 eggs, beaten

In a saucepan, mix together the mustard and vinegar. Let sit, covered, overnight on the kitchen counter (it will cook itself—you can see it bubble). In the morning, stir in the sugar and eggs. Cook, stirring over low heat, for 15 minutes. Store in a covered jar in the refrigerator.

MAKES 1½ CUPS

Herb Cheese Spread

    2 garlic cloves
    1 cup whipped butter, at room temperature
    2 large packages (8 ounces each) cream cheese, at room temperature
    1 teaspoon dried oregano
    ¼ teaspoon dried thyme
    ¼ teaspoon dried basil
    ¼ teaspoon dried marjoram

In a food processor, mince the garlic. Add all of the remaining ingredients and process until smooth. Place in a crock and refrigerate.

MAKES 2 CUPS

Simple Cheese Pizzas

    1 egg
    ¼ cup all-purpose flour
    ½ teaspoon salt
    ⅛ teaspoon pepper
    ¼ teaspoon dried oregano (optional)
    1 cup low-fat milk
    1 cup grated cheddar, Monterey Jack or mozzarella cheese

Preheat the oven to 400 degrees. Oil a pie plate.

In a food processor or blender, combine the egg, flour, salt, pepper, oregano and ½ cup of the milk. Mix thoroughly. Add the remaining ½ cup milk and mix again. Reserving 1 tablespoon for later, add the cheese.

Pour the mixture into the prepared pie plate. Bake for about 30 minutes, or until the edges are brown. Remove the "pizza" from the oven and sprinkle the reserved cheese over it (or add another kind of cheese, such as Parmesan). Place under the broiler for 1 to 2 minutes (watch carefully so that it doesn't burn), or until the cheese melts.

The result is a version of pizza that also tastes terrific cold. Make it on Sunday and slice a piece for your child's lunch box the next day.

MAKES 4 TO 6 SLICES

Yogurt Pancakes

1 egg
1 cup plain yogurt, blended or beaten until completely smooth
2 tablespoons safflower oil
1 cup all-purpose flour
1 tablespoon sugar
1 teaspoon baking powder
½ teaspoon baking soda
½ teaspoon salt
Vegetable oil, for frying

In a large bowl, whisk the egg, yogurt and safflower oil together. Add the flour, sugar, baking powder, baking soda and salt and mix well.

Lightly coat a skillet with oil. Make the pancakes as follows: Drop a tablespoon of batter in the pan. When bubbles appear, turn the pancake over and continue to cook until the underside is browned.

Cool, roll each up and fasten with a toothpick or refrigerate until needed.

MAKES 10 SMALL PANCAKES

Provolone Crisps

1½ cups shredded provolone cheese (about 6 ounces)
½ cup grated romano cheese
½ cup (1 stick) butter, at room temperature
Few drops of hot pepper sauce
1 cup all-purpose flour
1 teaspoon dried oregano, crushed
½ teaspoon paprika
¼ teaspoon salt
1 cup uncooked quick or old-fashioned oats

In a bowl, blend together the cheeses (reserve about 1 tablespoon romano), butter, pepper sauce and 3 tablespoons water. Add the flour, oregano, paprika, salt and oats and mix well. Form into a roll and wrap in plastic. Refrigerate for at least 4 hours.

Preheat the oven to 400 degrees. Butter a baking sheet.

Cut the roll into ⅛-inch slices and sprinkle with the reserved romano cheese. Place on the prepared baking sheet. Bake for 10 minutes, or until lightly browned.

Remove from the sheet and cool on a wire rack.

The dough will keep, stored air tight in the refrigerator, for a week.

MAKES 8 TO 12 CRISPS

✪

Yogurt Pancakes are terrific cold. If your child likes pancakes with jam, spread them with just a little of his or her favorite flavor (too much will drip out of the roll), then roll up as before.

★

Many meat and cheese sandwiches work well melted. Just spray vegetable spray on a small skillet and place the sandwich in it. Cook over low heat until the bottom is lightly browned. Turn over and brown the other side. Remove from the pan with a spatula and wrap in aluminum foil. Sandwiches that work well made this way include Pastrami and Cheese, Salami and Cheese, and Ham and Cheese.

FISH

SALMON SANDWICHES
TOMATO/SALMON BALLS
SALMON PATTIES
SNAPPER STICKS
TUNA SWIRLS
TUNA-NUT MUFFINS
TUNA SUNFLOWERS
TUNA PASTA SALAD

Salmon Sandwiches

1 can (15½ ounces) pink salmon, drained
1 package (4 ounces) whipped cream
    cheese, or 1 small package (3 ounces)
    regular cream cheese
¼ teaspoon liquid hickory smoke
2 tablespoons chopped chives
1 tablespoon chopped parsley
2 tablespoons fresh lemon juice
    Chopped walnuts (optional)
2 or 3 slices whole wheat bread

In a bowl, mix together all of the ingredients except the bread. Cover and refrigerate overnight.

In the morning, cut the crusts off the bread. Cut into shapes with cookie cutters. Toast lightly. Spread with some of the salmon mixture to make a single- or double-decker sandwich. Wrap in plastic.

Tomato/Salmon Balls

1 can (15½ ounces) pink salmon, drained
1 small package (3 ounces) cream cheese
¼ teaspoon liquid hickory smoke
2 tablespoons chopped chives
1 tablespoon chopped parsley
2 tablespoons fresh lemon juice
¼ cup chopped walnuts (optional)
1 pint cherry tomatoes, hollowed out from
    the stem end

In a bowl, mix together all of the ingredients except the tomatoes. Cover and chill.

Fill each cherry tomato with a teaspoon of the salmon mixture. Flatten at the top with a knife. If you have time, refrigerate for 10 minutes or so.

Wrap the tomatoes in foil and put in the lunch box.

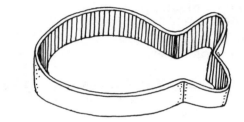 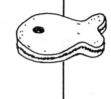

Salmon Patties

1 can (15½ ounces) pink salmon, drained
½ cup minced onion
10 saltine crackers, crushed
1 egg, beaten
2 tablespoons butter or margarine

In a bowl, combine the salmon, onion, crackers and egg. Mix to bind well.

Melt the butter in a skillet. Shape the salmon mixture into patties and fry until lightly browned. Cool and wrap in aluminum foil. These patties freeze well.

MAKES 6 TO 8 SALMON PATTIES

✿
If you have a fish-shaped cookie cutter, use it to turn the Salmon Sandwiches into a little fish.

✿
Peel and hollow out a cucumber. Let dry, stuff with salmon salad (from the Tomato/Salmon Balls recipe), then cut into cucumber rings.

✿
To make Tomato/Tuna Balls, simply substitute 1 can (12½ ounces) tuna for the salmon.

★
A TUNA SALAD VARIATION

1 6½ ounce can white tuna packed in water, drained
2 tablespoons light mayonnaise
1 teaspoon sugar (the miracle ingredient)
2 tablespoons pickle relish

Place the tuna in a food processor and process, pulsing on and off. Add the mayonnaise and sugar and pulse a couple more times. Place in a small bowl and stir in the pickle relish.

Spread on your favorite bread and enjoy.

Snapper Sticks

4 ounces firm fresh red snapper
Fresh lemon juice
Oil, for frying

Batter:

¾ cup all-purpose flour
1½ teaspoons baking powder
⅛ teaspoon salt
¼ cup milk
3 tablespoons vegetable oil

Cut the fish into strips about 2 inches long and ½- to ¾-inch wide. Sprinkle both sides with lemon juice.

Pour enough oil into a skillet to reach a depth of ½ inch. Set over low heat.

Meanwhile, prepare the batter: Combine the flour, baking powder and salt in a bowl. Whisk in the milk, oil and ¼ cup water; mix until smooth.

Increase the heat under the skillet. When the oil sizzles, dip the fish pieces in the batter and place in the pan. Fry until golden brown on both sides. Drain on paper towels. Cover and refrigerate.

In the morning, reheat the fish sticks in the toaster oven and wrap in aluminum foil.

MAKES 6 TO 8 STICKS

Tuna Swirls

1 can (12½ ounces) tuna packed in water (unsalted, if possible), drained
2 tablespoons mayonnaise or other spread
½ onion, chopped
1 small sweet pickle, chopped
Dash of liquid hickory smoke
¼ teaspoon fresh lemon juice
3 slices whole wheat bread
Dab of butter or margarine

In a bowl, combine the tuna, mayonnaise, onion, pickle, liquid smoke and lemon juice. Cover and refrigerate.

In the morning, cut the crusts off the bread and flatten each slice with a rolling pin (be careful not to roll so hard that you tear the bread).

Spread a thin layer of the tuna filling on the bread. Lay the bread slices out on a slightly dampened cloth and roll up as you would a jelly roll. Seal each seam with a dab of butter.

The result is a tuna roll that looks much like a jelly roll. Three will be plenty for most children under 13.

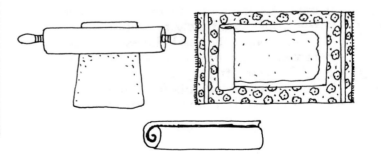

Tuna-Nut Muffins

   1 can (12½ ounces) tuna packed in water,
     drained
   ½ cup chopped unsalted peanuts or walnuts
   2 to 3 tablespoons mayonnaise
   1 cup chopped pickles (any kind)
   1 or 2 English muffins, lightly toasted

In a bowl, lightly blend the tuna, nuts, mayonnaise and pickles (do not put in the food processor or the texture will be too smooth). Cover and refrigerate.

In the morning, spread the mixture on the toasted English muffins and wrap.

Tuna Sunflowers

   1 can (12½ ounces) tuna packed in water,
     drained
   ½ cup shelled sunflower seeds
   1 small onion, chopped
   ½ teaspoon dried basil
   ½ cup plain low-fat yogurt
   2 slices whole wheat bread, egg bread or
     raisin bread

In a bowl, mix together all of the ingredients except the bread. If you are preparing this ahead of time, pack in a container and store in the refrigerator. If you are making it in the morning, put it in the refrigerator long enough to set (about 30 minutes).

Cut the crusts off the bread. Cut with a flower-shaped cookie cutter. Spread one slice with the tuna mixture and cover with the other.

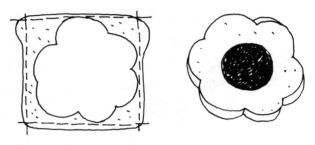

Tuna Pasta Salad

   2 eggs, hard-cooked and sliced
   1 cup steamed broccoli florets
   1 tomato, chopped
   2 cups cooked fusilli pasta
   1 cup tuna packed in water, drained
   ½ red bell pepper, chopped
   ½ cup steamed chopped green beans
   ½ cup kidney beans (optional—but
     nutritious)
   ½ cup chopped jicama (optional)
   ¼ cup chopped scallions
   ¼ cup vinaigrette dressing

In a bowl, combine all of the ingredients and toss to coat with the vinaigrette (a ranch dressing is also good on this). Cover and refrigerate.

When ready to pack a lunch, place a portion in a container and cover.

✪

You can also substitute plain yogurt for mayonnaise in all of the tuna and salmon recipes.

★

Betty Kerpen loves this tuna and pasta combination. Her hint: put half of the dressing on before you chill the salad. It marinates the vegetables and makes it even better. Then put the rest on when you are ready to eat (or are packing the lunch).

FRUITS

- AMBROSIA SALAD
- APPLE-BANANA SANDWICH
- APPLE KABOBS
- APPLE BUTTER
- DRIED FRUIT BITES
- FRUIT SPEARS
- STRAWBERRIES AND CREAM
- BANANA-SNOW PEA CRUNCHES

Ambrosia Salad

2 cups pineapple chunks (if canned, use
    juice-packed and drain well)
2 bananas, sliced
1 to 2 small apples, peeled, cored and
    chopped
2 oranges, peeled, sectioned and cut into
    pieces
2 cups strawberries, sliced
2 peaches, peeled, stoned and sliced
    (if not in season, you can use canned
    peaches, but drain well)
1 cup seedless grapes
½ cup raisins (optional)
¼ cup honey
1 cup plain or vanilla yogurt
½ teaspoon vanilla extract
2 cups miniature marshmallows (optional)
    Shredded coconut (optional)

In a large bowl, mix together all of the fruits.

Mix the honey, yogurt and vanilla. Pour the dressing over
the fruit and toss to coat. Add the marshmallows and
toss again. Cover and chill.

In the morning, place a portion of the salad in a small
container, sprinkle on the coconut and seal.

Apple-Banana Sandwich

2 slices whole wheat bread
    Butter
1 apple, peeled, cored and thinly sliced
½ banana, sliced
    Pinch of brown sugar
    Pinch of ground cinnamon

Toast the bread lightly. Butter one slice. Cover that slice
with apples and bananas and sprinkle with the brown
sugar and cinnamon.

Put in the toaster oven and broil for 1 minute. Don't over-
toast the bread—it should be fairly soft.

Take out of the toaster oven, cover with the other piece
of toast and wrap in aluminum foil.

Apple Kabobs

1 apple, peeled, cored and cubed
¼ cup fresh lemon juice
1 cup cubed Monterey Jack cheese
    (or cheddar or Swiss)

Dip the apple cubes in the lemon juice (it makes the apple
taste delicious and it keeps it from getting brown).
Alternate cubes of apple and cheese on small wooden
skewers.

Wrap in plastic wrap and chill until ready to put into the
lunch box.

MAKES 4 KABOBS

★ *Marc Gilbar makes his own
fresh orange juice every
morning and packs it in a
thermos for lunch. His
secret is to use fresh
oranges and a drop of
fresh lemon juice.*

✪ *For small kids, break off
the sharp tip of the skewer
when you make Apple
Kabobs.*

✪

*Variation on a theme—
make Strawberry Butter.
Place 1 cup (2 sticks)
of butter or margarine
in the food processor.
Add 2 cups chopped
strawberries. Blend.
That's it! It is superb on
plain or banana bread!*

★

*Dates and figs are very
high in potassium. It is
easy to blend these into
peanut butter in your food
processor, then stuff into
celery sticks. The extra
nutritional values are
great—and your kids
will never know.*

Apple Butter

**4 pounds tart apples, cored and quartered
   (about 10 cups)
½ cup cider vinegar
1 cup apple cider
2 cups packed brown sugar
2 teaspoons ground cinammon
1 teaspoon ground cloves
½ teaspoon ground allspice
   Juice and grated zest of 2 lemons**

In a saucepan, combine the apples, vinegar and apple cider. Cook over medium heat until soft.

Press through a food mill and return the puree to the saucepan.

Stir in the sugar, spices, lemon juice and lemon zest. Cook, stirring occasionally, over low heat until the apples are dark brown, about 3 hours. The liquid will cook out. Or you can make it the way we make applesauce (page 71).

If you desire, smooth the apple butter in the food processor, pulsing on and off. Don't overprocess or it will become too watery.

MAKES 2 TO 3 CUPS

Dried Fruit Bites

Dried fruit has a lot of potassium and calcium—so this is a surprisingly nutritious treat.

**1 small package (3 ounces) cream cheese,
   at room temperature
½ cup ricotta cheese
1 teaspoon vanilla extract
   As many dried fruits (apricots, figs,
   cherries, dates) as your child will eat
2 tablespoons chopped pistachio nuts
   (or any others you have at home)**

Blend the cheeses together in a food processor or blender. Add the vanilla and continue processing until the mixture is smooth. Cover and chill.

When you are making lunch, take each dried fruit and slice part of the way through on one side, forming a small pocket. Fill each piece with some of the mixture. (With apricots, spread the mixture on one slice, then top with another to form a tiny sandwich.) Sprinkle the top of each fruit with the nuts (stuff nuts inside the apricot sandwich).

Two to 3 pieces are enough for most kids.

Fruit Spears

Melon, cubed
Strawberries, when available
Pineapple, cubed
Grapes
Apricots, when available
Apple cubes (sprinkled with lemon juice
　to lessen browning)
Pear cubes (sprinkled with lemon juice)
Any other available fruit, in season
　or canned

Alternate pieces of the fruits you've decided to use on small wooden skewers. Wrap in plastic and chill until ready to go in the lunch box.

Strawberries and Cream

1 pint strawberries, washed and dried well,
　stems removed
½ teaspoon vanilla extract
½ cup yogurt (plain or flavored)

Halve the strawberries and place in a bowl. In another bowl, stir the vanilla into the yogurt. Pour over the strawberries and chill.

In the morning, spoon a portion into a plastic container and cover. Remember to include a plastic spoon.

Banana-Snow Pea Crunches

1 banana
1 teaspoon fresh lemon juice
1 cup cream cheese, at room temperature
　Chinese snow peas

Mash the banana with a fork and mix in the lemon juice to keep the banana from turning brown. Mix in the cream cheese (do this with a spoon or fork—the food processor will make the mixture too liquid).

Cut off the ends of the snow peas just at the tips. Use a paring knife to open each snow pea on one long side. Spread some of the mixture into each snow pea with a butter knife. They will look like little boats. Wrap in plastic wrap.

✪

You can also use tuna or egg salad to fill the snow peas.

★

To make "fake" sour cream, blend together cottage cheese and a few drops of lemon juice in your food processor or electric blender.

★

The combined flavors of berries, vanilla and yogurt are unbeatable for a lunch-box treat. Depending on which fresh berries are in season, you can eat this dish all year round. Try it with blueberries, boysen-berries, blackberries or raspberries. If none are in the market, you can use frozen berries, but be sure to defrost and drain well before mixing with the vanilla and yogurt (other-wise it will be too watery).

MEATS/POULTRY

BARBECUED TERIYAKI
  SPARERIBS
CHINESE CHICKEN
  SALAD SANDWICHES
CHICKEN DRUMMETTES
MOM'S CHICKEN SALAD
CHICKEN FAJITA PITA
CLUB SANDWICH
CRUNCHY CHICKEN SALAD
SESAME CHICKEN
DATE-A-BACON
EASY CHICKEN

MEREDITH'S SUNDAY
  NIGHT ROAST CHICKEN
WONTONS
TENDERLOIN SANDWICHES
MOZZARELLA TURKEY SALAD
ALICE WATERS'S PASTA SALAD
MINI MEAT LOAF POCKETS
PORKY AND BUGS BUNNIES
ROAST BEEF WRAPPERS
TURKEY HOT DOGS
HAM ROLLS
TURKEY ON A STICK

Barbecued Teriyaki Spareribs

1 pound pork spareribs

Teriyaki Sauce:

  ½ cup Japanese soy sauce
  2 tablespoons dry sherry
  3 tablespoons sugar
  2 tablespoons grated fresh ginger
  1 garlic clove, mashed

Parboil the spareribs for 25 minutes.

Meanwhile, combine all of the teriyaki sauce ingredients in the blender and mix. You will have about ½ cup of sauce.

Drain the ribs and pat dry with paper towels. Place in a glass dish and coat with the sauce. Marinate in the sauce for 1 hour or more.

Broil the ribs, basting with the teriyaki sauce until nicely browned, crispy and well done. To store, cover and refrigerate.

In the morning, when you are ready to pack your child's lunch box, reheat the spareribs in a toaster oven. Wrap in aluminum foil. They are also tasty at room temperature.

Chinese Chicken Salad Sandwiches

  ¾ cup bean or alfalfa sprouts
  ¼ cup chopped canned bamboo shoots
  ¼ cup chopped cooked broccoli
  2 cups chopped broiled chicken
  1 teaspoon low-sodium soy sauce
  1 tablespoon chopped parsley
  2 tablespoons mayonnaise
  2 slices whole wheat bread, crusts removed

In a bowl, mix the sprouts, bamboo shoots, broccoli, chicken and soy sauce. Let it stand while you make breakfast (or if this is your Sunday night preparation, let it stand for about 15 minutes). When you are ready to use, drain well.

Stir in the parsley and mayonnaise. Spread a slice of bread with additional mayonnaise, butter or margarine. Top with a not-too-thick layer of the salad. Cover with another slice of bread.

Cut the sandwich with a chicken-shaped cookie cutter and there you have it—a Chinese Chicken Salad Sandwich! Refrigerate leftover salad, covered.

★ *If you have trouble cutting the Chinese Chicken Salad Sandwich, cut the bread before you put the mixture on it.*

✿

Any leftover Chicken Drummettes marinade will keep well, too. Simply freeze and reheat (bringing to a boil) when ready to use.

★

Laurie Burrows Grad, the well-known cookbook author, has her own easy, low-cal version of Chicken Drummettes:

3 to 4 tablespoons unsalted margarine
14 chicken drummettes
1 cup buttermilk
1½ cups unsweetened cereal crumbs

Preheat the oven to 400 degrees.

Melt the butter in a 9- x 13-inch baking dish. Dip the drummettes in the buttermilk and then in the crumbs, making sure to press the crumbs into the chicken. Place in the pan in a single layer.

Bake for 25 to 30 minutes, or until golden all over. Refrigerate.

In the morning, reheat in the toaster oven. Wrap in foil and pack in the lunch box.

Chicken Drummettes

½ cup packed brown sugar
½ cup low-sodium soy sauce
2 tablespoons mirin (sweet rice wine, optional—once this mixture is cooked, the alcohol will have evaporated)
Pinch of ground ginger
1 scallion, trimmed and minced
12 to 24 chicken drummettes (the upper part of the wing; your supermarket meat counter often has them packaged. If you can't find them, ask the butcher to put some together for you)

In a glass baking dish, combine all of the ingredients, except the chicken. Stir to dissolve the sugar. Add the chicken and marinate for 1 hour, turning from time to time.

When the chicken is almost finished marinating, preheat the oven to 350 degrees.

Drain the drummettes, reserving the marinade.

Bake the chicken, basting occasionally with the marinade, for 30 minutes, or until tender. The drummettes are delicious cold and taste even better the next day.

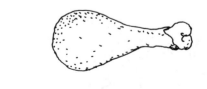

Mom's Chicken Salad

Mayonnaise:

2 egg yolks
1 tablespoon Dijon mustard
2 tablespoons raspberry vinegar
1½ cups vegetable oil
1 cup crumbled Roquefort cheese
Salt
Pepper

Salad:

4 poached chicken breasts
1 cup diced celery
1½ cups seedless grapes, halved
¾ cup chopped peanuts or pumpkin seeds

Make the mayonnaise: In a blender or food processor, combine the egg yolks, mustard and vinegar. Process for about 30 seconds. With the machine running, add the oil in a thin steady stream and beat until thick. Add the cheese and process until well combined but not smooth. Season to taste with salt and pepper.

Discard the skin from the chicken breasts and pull the meat off the bones in large chunks. Cut the meat into 1-inch chunks.

In a large bowl, combine the chicken, celery, grapes and peanuts. Add enough mayonnaise to cover and toss to coat the ingredients well. Cover and refrigerate until chilled. Pack in a plastic container or spread on a sandwich.

Chicken Fajita Pita

We don't know who first coined this name, but the Gilbar kids live for the lunch boxes holding our version of a Mexican taco.

> 1 **boneless and skinless chicken breast, broiled or quick fried**
> **Pinch of commercial fajita seasoning**
> **Shredded lettuce**
> 2 **slices tomato**
> 2 **slices cheddar cheese**
> 1 **pita bread**

You can use leftover chicken breast cut into strips, or, if you have the time in the morning, sauté a few strips of fresh chicken meat with the fajita seasoning. Slice one side of the pita bread to form a pocket. Fill the bread with the chicken and all of the remaining ingredients.

Club Sandwich

> 2 **slices whole wheat bread**
> **Butter, margarine or mayonnaise**
> 4 **slices chicken breast**
> 2 **slices medium-crisp bacon**
> 2 **slices tomato**
> 1 **slice cheddar cheese**
> 2 to 3 **pickle slices (optional)**

Toast the bread lightly. Spread with butter, margarine or mayonnaise on one side only. Arrange the sliced chicken, bacon, tomatoes, cheese and pickles on one piece of bread. Cover with the other slice of bread.

Cut the sandwich into 4 equal squares. Wrap tightly in foil to hold it together.

Crunchy Chicken Salad

> 1 **cup chopped cooked chicken (the meat from 2 legs and thighs)**
> 1 **tablespoon chopped onion**
> 2 **tablespoons chopped sweet pickles**
> **Dash of Worcestershire sauce**
> 1 **hard-cooked egg, chopped**
> ¼ **cup chopped cooked broccoli**
> 1 **tablespoon mayonnaise (you can use more)**
> 1 **tablespoon chopped parsley**
> **Salt and pepper**
> 1 **pita bread (regular, whole wheat or miniature)**

In a bowl, mix together all of the ingredients except the pita bread and season with salt and pepper to taste.

Cut into one side of the pita to make a pocket. Fill the pocket with chicken salad, but do not overstuff. Wrap in foil or plastic.

You can add minced dill or sweet pickle relish in the Chicken Fajita Pita.

If your child likes Russian dressing, pour 1 tablespoon into the pita after everything else is in it (more will soak the bread).

For extra fun, cut a piece of whole wheat bread and a piece of white bread to create a two-color sandwich. You can also get an hors d'oeuvre cutter (in any housewares store or hardware store) and cut out the center of the flower. Leave it out or flip the centers so the whole wheat one is in the white flower and vice versa.

Variations for stuffing Chicken Salad:
- stuff salad into pitas
- roll it up in tortillas
- core an apple and stuff with the salad

Here's a variation on that old cream cheese in celery recipe. After you fill a piece of celery with cream cheese, wrap it in a slice of ham or turkey and seal with a toothpick or dab of butter. You can also use this wrapping trick on vegetables or fruits— wrap a spear of melon or cucumber in a slice of ham.

For variety, you can add a crushed garlic clove and/or ½ teaspoon dried rosemary to the Easy Chicken marinade.

Sesame Chicken

6 chicken pieces (fresh, not frozen)
Dash of seasoned salt
Dash of pepper
Dash of paprika
¼ cup sesame seeds
1 cup all-purpose flour
Safflower or peanut oil, for frying

Wash and dry the chicken pieces.

Place the salt, pepper, paprika, sesame seeds and flour in a paper or plastic bag. Drop 2 to 3 chicken pieces into the bag and shake well, until the chicken is completely coated.

Heat oil (3 inches deep) in a deep fryer or chicken fryer, making sure the oil is very hot before you start cooking. Put in 3 pieces of chicken at a time and cook, uncovered, until golden brown on all sides (a breast takes about 15 minutes, so judge accordingly). Remove the chicken from the fryer and drain on paper towels. Keep the chicken warm while frying the remaining pieces.

Date-A-Bacon

The combination of the sweet taste of a date and the salty flavor of bacon is a favorite. Children up to the age of eight easily will eat four of these. If they're older than that, you're on your own!

6 bacon slices, cut crosswise in half
12 dates, pitted

Either fry the bacon, bake at 450 degrees or, the simplest method, microwave the strips until only half-cooked.

Wrap a piece of bacon around each date and fasten with a toothpick. Finish cooking the bacon (in the oven or pan), turning once, until crisp but not burned. Drain on paper towels and wrap in foil.

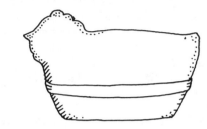

Easy Chicken

Juice of 1 lemon
¼ cup olive oil
¼ teaspoon pepper
¼ teaspoon salt
4 to 6 of your favorite chicken parts

In a large bowl, mix together the lemon juice, oil, pepper, and salt. Add the chicken parts and marinate for 1 hour.

Preheat the broiler.

Place the marinated chicken in a baking dish and broil for 20 minutes.

Prick the chicken with a knife to test for doneness (the juice should run clear). If the juice is pink, cook a little longer.

Meredith's Sunday Night Roast Chicken

This chicken is easy to make at the end of the weekend, perfect to keep for several days worth of chicken salad, chicken sandwiches, chicken kabobs, chicken rolls, chicken nuggets and the like.

1 whole roasting chicken (about
    5 pounds)
2 tablespoons olive oil
1 tablespoon Dijon mustard
½ lemon
1 bunch parsley
1 teaspoon dried thyme
2 garlic cloves, peeled
1 chicken liver
1 small carrot
1 onion, sliced
   Dash of salt and pepper

Preheat the oven to 400 degrees.

Wash and dry the chicken. Place it in a roasting pan. Brush the outside of the chicken with the olive oil and mustard. Squeeze the juice of the lemon on the chicken, inside and out. Place the squeezed lemon, parsley, thyme, garlic, chicken liver, carrot and onion in the cavity of the chicken. Sprinkle with salt and pepper. Cover loosely with aluminum foil. Bake for 30 minutes.

Reduce the heat to 350 degrees. Uncover and bake for 30 minutes more. To test for doneness, prick the chicken with a knife to see if the juice runs clear.

Store, covered, in the refrigerator, to use during the first part of the week.

Wontons

1 small can (8 ounces) water chestnuts or
    bamboo shoots, drained
½ pound ground lean pork or sirloin, cooked
1 tablespoon low-sodium soy sauce
1 tablespoon chopped scallions
¼ teaspoon garlic powder
1 package wonton skins (found in the
    refrigerated section of your grocery
    store; you'll need only half of the skins
    in the package for this recipe, but you
    can keep the rest, refrigerated)
1 egg, beaten
   Peanut or soy oil, for frying

Chop the water chestnuts or place in a food processor and process for 10 seconds. In a bowl, mix together the chopped water chestnuts, meat, soy sauce, scallions and garlic powder.

Cut the stack of wonton skins into 2-inch squares. With dampened fingers, separate the skins and arrange on a work surface. Put 1 teaspoon of the mixture on each wonton skin. Fold the skins over to make triangles. Moisten the edges with the beaten egg and pinch the edges together to close. Make sure the wontons are sealed.

Pour enough oil in a skillet to reach a depth of ¼ inch. Working in batches, fry the wontons, turning to brown on all sides. As each is browned, remove and drain on paper towels. Allow to cool. Cover and refrigerate.

PLUM SAUCE

1 cup plum jelly
½ cup chutney
1 tablespoon sugar
1 teaspoon any type
   vinegar

Combine the plum jelly and chutney in a food processor and pulse "on and off" until well mixed. Scrape into a saucepan. Stir in the sugar and vinegar. Cook, stirring constantly, for about 5 minutes, until thick.

Remove and put into a covered plastic container or glass jar. Refrigerate.

*MAKES ABOUT
1 CUP PLUM SAUCE*

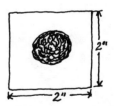

✪
You can also use leftover steak or roast beef. For variation, add roasted peppers, grilled onions or anything else your child might like in the bun.

✪
Fresh bread for fresh bread crumbs is most important in the Pasta Salad. So get a country-style bread and make bread crumbs in a food processor or blender. Put crumbs in a baking dish and place in oven, under low heat, until dry and crisp (but not brown). Reserve.

Tenderloin Sandwiches

This simple sandwich can be prepared in minutes.

1 pound beef tenderloin
Salt and pepper
Butter or margarine
Miniature hamburger buns

Slice the tenderloin into as many thin slices as you will need. Cut them into manageable sizes for a small sandwich. Season the meat with a little salt and pepper. Butter a skillet and quickly brown the slices of beef on each side. Let cool for a minute and put into the buns.

Wrap in aluminum foil or plastic.

MAKES 6 TO 8 SANDWICHES

Mozzarella Turkey Salad

2 cups diced mozzarella cheese
4 hard-cooked eggs, diced
1 cup diced baked turkey breast
¾ cup sour cream or plain non-fat yogurt
2 tablespoons Dijon mustard
1 tablespoon capers
2 tablespoons minced parsley
¼ cup minced scallions
½ teaspoon salt

In a bowl, mix together the cheese, eggs and turkey. Add the other ingredients and mix well. Cover and chill.

In the morning, spoon a portion of salad into a plastic container and cover.

Alice Waters's Pasta Salad

Alice Waters, owner of Chez Panisse restaurant in Berkeley, California, developed this recipe for the lunch box. It makes enough for 4 to 6 servings.

 4 cups yellow and red cherry tomatoes
1 handful fresh basil leaves, minced
1 large bunch parsley, minced
Salt and pepper
1 to 2 garlic cloves, minced
½ cup olive oil
4 cups fresh bread crumbs
8 ounces fusilli (pasta shaped like coiled springs)
8 ounces cooked ham, diced

Cut the tomatoes in half. In a bowl, combine the tomatoes with the basil and parsley. Add salt and pepper to taste. Set aside.

Combine the garlic and the oil in a large skillet over medium heat. Add the bread crumbs and sauté until golden brown. Pour into a bowl and set aside.

Cook the pasta in a pot of boiling water until al dente. Drain and turn into a large bowl. Add the tomatoes, bread crumbs and ham. Toss well. Serve immediately or refrigerate.

You can prepare this recipe and serve it hot for dinner or at room temperature, reserving any that is left over in a plastic container in the refrigerator. The next morning, just put the container in your child's lunch box to provide a cold luncheon salad.

Mini Meat Loaf Pockets

You haven't tasted fabulous meat loaf until you've had this! Even the pickiest of kids who absolutely and positively detest meat loaf will love this one. It is juicy and tasty—a treat!

 1 pound lean ground beef
1 egg
½ cup dry bread crumbs
½ onion, chopped
½ cup ready-made spaghetti sauce
    Dash of Worcestershire sauce
¼ teaspoon liquid hickory smoke or a
    dash of hickory powder
    Pinch of dried marjoram
    Pinch of dried thyme
1 tablespoon chopped parsley
1 pita bread
    Avocado slices (optional)
    Tomato slices (optional)

Preheat the oven to 350 degrees. Butter either 2 mini loaf pans or 1 small loaf pan (about 7½ x 3½ inches).

Place all of the ingredients except the bread, avocado and tomatoes in a large bowl. Mix well.

Shape the meat mixture into a loaf and put in the pans. Bake for 40 minutes. (If mini loaf pans are used, check for doneness after 30 minutes and take care that the loaves don't dry out.) Let cool to room temperature. Cover and refrigerate to use later.

In the morning, cut 2 slices of the meat loaf. Open a pita at one end and place the meat loaf in the pocket. Add a slice of avocado and tomato, if your child likes them, and you've got a pita pocket.

Porky and Bugs Bunnies

4 slices whole wheat bread
    Mayonnaise, butter, margarine or
        mustard (optional)
2 slices cooked ham
2 slices Swiss or cheddar cheese
4 raisins (optional)

Cut the crusts off the bread. Spread one side of the bread slices with the mayonnaise (you may also leave the bread dry). On each of 2 slices of bread, place a slice of ham and a slice of cheese. Cover with the remaining 2 slices of bread.

Cut through the sandwich with a bunny-shaped cookie cutter. If desired, cut tiny holes in the bread and use raisins to make bunny eyes.

☻ *Try making the Meat Loaf in a buttered muffin tin. Bake for 25 to 30 minutes. Wrap and refrigerate. When packing for the lunch box, wrap in aluminum foil (you don't need pita pockets for the meat muffins).*

**NANA'S
MEAT LOAF GLAZE**

1 cup tomato sauce
1 8-ounce jar apricot
    preserves
2 tablespoons
    Worcestershire sauce

Heat all the ingredients in a saucepan. Pour over the meat loaf ½ hour before it's done.

MAKES 2 CUPS

☻ *You can flatten the Porky and Bugs Bunnies bread slices with a rolling pin.*

Roast Beef Wrappers

Richard Krause, chef at Wolfgang Puck's Chinois on Main in Los Angeles, California, devised this favorite.

1 tablespoon Dijon mustard
1 tablespoon mayonnaise
6 thin slices rare roast beef
1 carrot, peeled and cut into 3 long thin "sticks"
1 celery rib, cut into 3 long thin strips

Spread the mustard and mayonnaise on the roast beef slices. Wrap each stick of carrot and celery in a slice of meat. Wrap in foil or plastic and chill.

Make only as many as your child will eat.

Turkey Hot Dogs

1 turkey hot dog
1 soft tortilla (either corn or flour)
Mustard or cranberry sauce (optional)

Cook the hot dog for 3 to 4 minutes in boiling water; cool.

Place the hot dog on a tortilla and spread with mustard or cranberry sauce, if desired. Roll the tortilla around the hot dog and secure with a toothpick. Wrap in foil.

Ham Rolls

¼ cup sunflower seeds
1 tablespoon sesame seeds
¼ cup mayonnaise
1 teaspoon fresh lemon juice
1 apple, peeled, cored and finely chopped
   Pinch of ground cinammon
2 slices boiled ham (about 4- by 6-inch slices)
2 hot dog rolls, preferably whole wheat

In a bowl, mix together the sunflower seeds, sesame seeds, mayonnaise, lemon juice and apple. Add the cinnamon to taste.

Place the ham slices on a cutting board. Spread each with half of the apple mixture. Roll up each slice.

Toast the hot dog rolls. Place a ham roll in each. Wrap in foil.

Turkey on a Stick

2 slices smoked turkey
Butter or margarine
Mustard
Mayonnaise
2 bread sticks

Spread each slice of turkey with butter, mustard and mayonnaise. Roll one slice around each bread stick. Dab a bit of butter on the end to seal the edges. Now you have a child's nutritious version of the lollipop.

✪ Roll ham around other vegetables such as asparagus, green beans, sliced pepper, celery, carrots or any vegetable your child might like.

✪ A hungry or older child may eat 2 Ham Rolls, but a young child (under 8) will probably eat only 1.

★ On cold winter days, why not warm your child's heart by sending hot chocolate or hot apple cider (add a pinch of cinnamon and a few drops of lemon juice before heating) in a thermos.

PEANUTS/PEANUT BUTTER

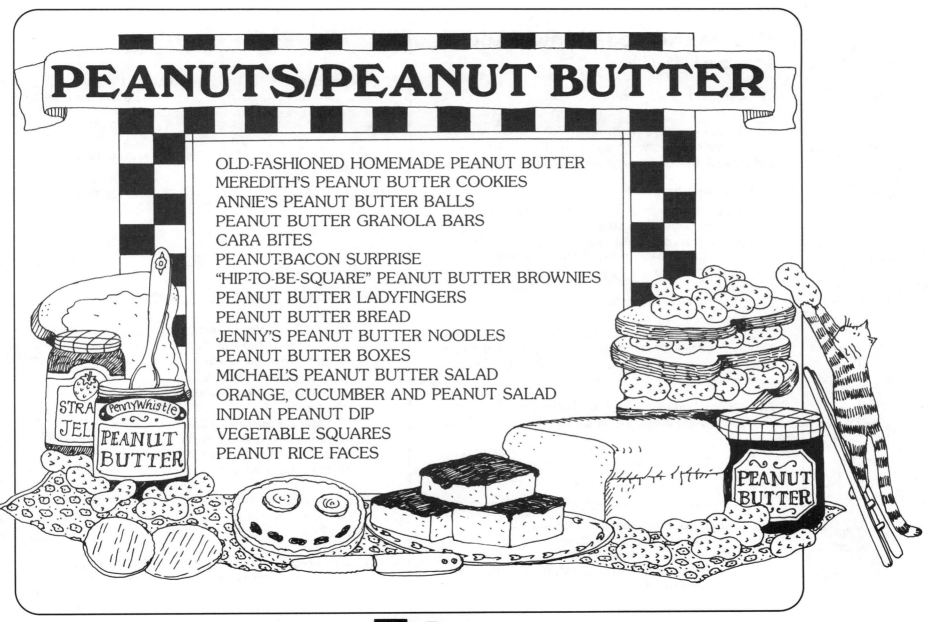

OLD-FASHIONED HOMEMADE PEANUT BUTTER
MEREDITH'S PEANUT BUTTER COOKIES
ANNIE'S PEANUT BUTTER BALLS
PEANUT BUTTER GRANOLA BARS
CARA BITES
PEANUT-BACON SURPRISE
"HIP-TO-BE-SQUARE" PEANUT BUTTER BROWNIES
PEANUT BUTTER LADYFINGERS
PEANUT BUTTER BREAD
JENNY'S PEANUT BUTTER NOODLES
PEANUT BUTTER BOXES
MICHAEL'S PEANUT BUTTER SALAD
ORANGE, CUCUMBER AND PEANUT SALAD
INDIAN PEANUT DIP
VEGETABLE SQUARES
PEANUT RICE FACES

✪

Peanuts with red skins may be used in the Peanut Butter. (Do not confuse skins with outer shells!) The resulting red flecks do not affect the flavor.

★

Meredith hates to waste anything—she always finds a good use for leftovers. Here's one for leftover peanut butter: Take a foot-long 3- to 4-inch in diameter log, and screw an eye-hook into one end. With a knife, spread the entire log with peanut butter. Now, roll it in unsalted sunflower seeds and hang as a birdfeeder.

Old-Fashioned Homemade Peanut Butter

The Georgia Peanut Commission has come up with a make-it-at-home peanut butter recipe that is easy and delicious. Actually, there are two recipes which we have reproduced here—one for use with an electric blender, the other for a food processor.

Electric Blender Method:

    1 cup roasted shelled peanuts (with or
        without red skins)
    1½ teaspoons peanut oil
    ¼ teaspoon salt (omit if salted peanuts
        are used)

Place the ingredients in a blender. With the lid secured, blend until mixture becomes paste-like or spreadable, 3 to 4 minutes. If necessary, stop the machine and use a rubber spatula to scrape down the sides of the container. Continue blending until the desired consistency is obtained.

Note: For chunk-style peanut butter, stir in ¼ cup chopped roasted peanuts after the blending is completed.

*MAKES ½ CUP SMOOTH OR
¾ CUP CHUNKY PEANUT BUTTER*

Food Processor Method:

    2 cups roasted shelled peanuts (with
        or without red skins)
    1 tablespoon peanut oil
    ½ teaspoon salt (omit if salted peanuts
        are used)

Using the metal blade, process the ingredients continuously for 2 to 3 minutes. The ground peanuts will form a ball which will slowly disappear. Continue to process until the desired smoothness is obtained. If necessary, stop the machine and scrape down the sides of the container with a rubber spatula.

Note: For chunky-style peanut butter, stir in ½ cup chopped roasted peanuts after the processing is completed.

*MAKES 1 CUP SMOOTH OR
1½ CUPS CHUNKY PEANUT BUTTER*

Meredith's Peanut Butter Cookies

    ¾ cup (1½ sticks) butter or margarine, at
        room temperature
    1 cup granulated sugar
    ½ cup packed brown sugar
    1 teaspoon vanilla extract
    2 eggs
    2 cups all-purpose flour
    1 teaspoon baking soda
    1 cup chunky peanut butter
    1 cup chopped lightly salted peanuts

In the bowl of an electric mixer, cream together the butter, granulated and brown sugars, and vanilla until fluffy. Add the eggs and beat well.

In another bowl, combine the flour and baking soda. Add to the creamed mixture, scraping the sides of the bowl.

Beat in the peanut butter and peanuts. Mix well. Cover and refrigerate the dough for 1 hour.

Preheat the oven to 350 degrees.

Drop the dough by teaspoonfuls onto an ungreased baking sheet. Flatten with the tines of a fork, making a crisscross pattern. Bake for 10 minutes. Let cool. Store in a covered cookie jar.

Annie's Peanut Butter Balls

½ cup dates
1 cup smooth peanut butter
2 tablespoons honey
1 tablespoon butter
1 cup instant powdered milk
1 cup chopped peanuts
1 cup shredded coconut

Chop the dates by placing them in the container of a food processor and pulsing on and off. Don't overprocess.

Transfer the dates to a mixing bowl and add all the other ingredients except the coconut. Stir until the mixture is gooey in consistency, then pull off small pieces in your hands and shape them into 1-inch balls. Roll each ball in coconut until thoroughly coated. Store the balls in a covered container in the freezer.

In the morning, take out two or three, place in a plastic bag and send to school. The balls will defrost by lunchtime.

Peanut Butter Granola Bars

3 cups granola
1 cup chopped dried apricots
½ cup chopped peanuts
½ cup sunflower seeds
½ cup smooth peanut butter
2 cups orange honey
2 eggs
4 tablespoons butter or margarine

In a mixing bowl, combine the granola, apricots, peanuts and sunflower seeds. Set aside.

In a nonstick saucepan, combine the peanut butter and honey. Mix with a wooden spoon until smooth and liquid. Beat the eggs and add, one at a time, stirring continuously, until the mixture begins to boil. Remove from the heat and stir in the butter. Allow to cool.

Butter a 9-inch square pan or dish.

Pour the honey and peanut butter mixture over the granola mixture and stir to coat thoroughly. Spoon into the prepared pan. Refrigerate for at least a couple of hours.

Cut into 1- or 2-inch bars. One per lunch box is a super treat.

MAKES ABOUT 24 BARS

✪
Store the Granola Bars in the refrigerator on a plate between two sheets of waxed paper. It will keep them fresher longer.

★
When Charlotte Newman moved to Cleveland, Ohio, her peanut butter balls developed a Buckeye twist:

CHARLOTTE'S BUCKEYE BALLS

1 jar (18 ounces) peanut butter
¼ to ½ cup honey
2¼ cups powdered milk
1 cup chocolate chips, melted

In a food processor, blend the peanut butter and honey. Add the powdered milk and blend again. Shape the balls as described in the recipe above and dip half of each ball into the melted chocolate. Let chocolate dry, store in a covered container and refrigerate or freeze.

★

Besides her computer, Cara Familian, a Harvard freshman, is taking her favorite recipe for lunch (one that she has been making for herself and her little brother, Seth, for eight years). Her secret: a triple decker peanut butter sandwich. Take a slice of bread and spread with jelly. Cover with another slice and spread with peanut butter, topped with slices of banana. Cover with another slice of bread, cut into squares and wrap.

✪

Add pickles to this lunch box, if your child likes them. The salty taste is a good complement to the Peanut-Bacon Surprise.

✪

Apples are delicious with the Peanut-Bacon Surprise. If your child likes them, you can slice half an apple, dip the slices in lemon juice, and then arrange on the sandwich. Or, you can just add an apple to the lunch box.

Cara Bites

1 cup fresh bread crumbs
2 cups peanut butter (crunchy or smooth)
3 tablespoons safflower oil
24 Triscuit crackers

Preheat the oven to 350 degrees. Cover a baking sheet with aluminum foil.

Place the bread crumbs on a plate; set aside.

In a small saucepan, combine the peanut butter and oil and stir with a wooden spoon until warm (but not boiling).

Using metal tongs, dip each cracker into the peanut butter until covered and then into the bread crumbs. When done with each, place on the baking sheet to dry in the oven for 15 minutes.

Store in a covered container. Wrap in aluminum foil in the morning.

Peanut-Bacon Surprise

2 slices raisin bread
  Crunchy peanut butter
2 slices medium-crisp bacon

Toast the bread lightly; let cool. Cut off the crusts.

Spread one slice with peanut butter and arrange the bacon on top. Cover with the second slice of bread and wrap.

"Hip-To-Be-Square" Peanut Butter Brownies

This recipe is reprinted courtesy of the Peanut Advisory Board, from their Adults Only Peanut Butter Lovers Official Cookie Handbook.

Brownies:

2 ounces unsweetened chocolate, coarsely chopped
½ cup creamy peanut butter
¼ pound (1 stick) unsalted butter
2 eggs
1 cup sugar
1 teaspoon vanilla extract
¾ cup all-purpose flour
  Pinch of salt
¼ cup sour cream

Chocolate Icing:

1 cup sugar
1 tablespoon light corn syrup
⅓ cup milk
2 ounces unsweetened chocolate, coarsely chopped
2 tablespoons unsalted butter
½ teaspoon vanilla extract

Preheat the oven to 325 degrees. Butter and flour an 8-inch square baking pan.

Make the brownies: In a double-boiler over simmering water, melt together the chocolate, peanut butter and butter. Set aside to cool.

In a bowl, beat together the eggs, sugar and vanilla until light and fluffy. Now beat in the chocolate mixture. Stir in the flour, salt and sour cream.

Pour the batter into the prepared pan. Bake for 30 minutes. Remove to cool on a rack.

Meanwhile, make the icing: In a heavy small saucepan, combine the sugar, corn syrup, milk and chocolate. Stirring constantly, bring to a boil. Remove from heat.

Beat in the butter and vanilla and continue beating until cooled slightly.

Spread over the cooled brownies. Cut into bars.

MAKES 16 BROWNIES

Peanut Butter Ladyfingers

8 dried figs
2 cups smooth peanut butter
4 ladyfingers, chilled

In a food processor or blender, process the figs and peanut butter to a fairly smooth paste.

If they are not already precut, slice open 4 ladyfingers. Spread one half with the peanut butter mixture and cover with the other half. Wrap in plastic wrap.

Peanut Butter Bread

This bread is very nutritious—full of vitamin A, potassium and calcium.

½ **cup chunky peanut butter**
½ **cup orange or plain honey**
3 **tablespoons vegetable oil**
2 **eggs**
½ **cup grated carrots**
2 **bananas, mashed**
¼ **cup low-fat milk**
¼ **teaspoon ground cinnamon**
¼ **teaspoon ground cloves**
¼ **teaspoon ground nutmeg**
1 **teaspoon vanilla extract**
Pinch of salt
1 **teaspoon baking powder**
1 **teaspoon baking soda**
1¾ **cups whole wheat flour**

Preheat the oven to 300 degrees. Butter a 9- x 5-inch loaf pan.

In a bowl, blend together the peanut butter, honey, oil, eggs, carrots and bananas. Add the milk, spices, vanilla, salt, baking powder, baking soda and flour. Blend together well.

Pour the batter into the prepared pan. Bake for 1 hour and 15 minutes, or until a toothpick inserted in the center comes out clean. Cool the bread on a wire rack.

Use plain or top with a spread.

Some kids are just starving when they finish school. Adrienne Horwitch always picked her kids up holding a bag for each, carefully wrapped and closed with a sticker, containing 3 mini ritz cracker "sandwiches" filled with peanut butter. It gave them immediate energy—and they still remember Mom's thoughtfulness today, more than 10 years later!

Before Pam Lyons measures peanut butter, she coats her measuring cup with oil. That makes the peanut butter slide out easily.

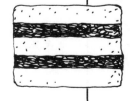

When Melissa and Jesse Bochco were growing up, mom Barbara had her own treat for their lunch boxes. She would take a large apple, core it, peel it and cut it into 4 pieces. She then spread peanut butter on all the center sections, reassembled the apple and wrapped it tightly in foil so it wouldn't turn brown. Yet another favorite trick was to stuff the apple with cheese slices.

Jenny's Peanut Butter Noodles

This is the salad Jennifer Brokaw chose as her favorite lunchtime salad.

> 1 package (8 ounces) linguine pasta
> 2 to 3 tablespoons peanut butter
> ½ teaspoon salt
> 2 tablespoons soy sauce
> 1 tablespoon Oriental sesame oil
> 1 teaspoon sugar
> ½ teaspoon white wine vinegar
> 2 garlic cloves, crushed
> 1 teaspoon chopped grated onion

Cook the linguine according to the directions on the package. Drain.

Meanwhile, in a large bowl, mix all of the remaining ingredients together.

Add the linguine to the sauce and toss to coat well. When ready to pack the lunch, put a portion in a small container and cover.

Peanut Butter Boxes

> 1 cup peanut butter
> 2 tablespoons mayonnaise
> 1 tablespoon apricot jam or currant jelly
> 3 tablespoons crumbled bacon
> 3 slices Banana Bread (see recipe, page 26)

Mix together the peanut butter, mayonnaise, jam and bacon.

Spread the mixture on a slice of bread. Cover with another slice. Spread again with the mixture and cover with another slice of bread. Cut the banana bread into a square or box shape. If your child is small, cut into smaller boxes. Store the remainder of the spread in a covered jar in the refrigerator.

Michael's Peanut Butter Salad

Here is a peanut butter salad inspired by one made for us by Michael Roberts, chef at Trump's restaurant in Los Angeles.

> ½ cup smooth peanut butter
> 1 teaspoon Oriental sesame oil
> ½ teaspoon cider vinegar
> 2 cups cooked green beans
> 2 cups thinly sliced jicama
> 1 cup grated carrots
> 1 cup cooked green peas

In a bowl, mix together the peanut butter, oil and vinegar. Set the sauce aside.

In another bowl, mix together all of the vegetables. Pour on the sauce and toss. Cover and chill if making the night before.

If you make it in the morning, place about 1 cup of salad in a plastic container. Cover tightly. Include some pita slices or pita chips to eat with the salad.

Vegetable Squares

½ cup smooth peanut butter
2 carrots, peeled and grated
½ cup raisins
2 tablespoons mayonnaise
2 slices bread

In a bowl, mix together all of the ingredients except the bread. Be sure you have enough mayonnaise to bind the ingredients but not so much as to make the mixture runny.

Toast the bread lightly. Spread the mixture on one side and cover. Cut each slice into small squares and wrap.

Indian Peanut Dip

½ cup smooth peanut butter
1 teaspoon chopped onion
¼ cup lemon juice
1 tablespoon soy sauce
Pinch of garlic powder
½ teaspoon ground coriander

In your food processor, mix together all the ingredients until smooth. Store in a covered container in the refrigerator. In the morning, place about 2 tablespoons of dip in a plastic container and cover. Send to school with some cut-up vegetables (carrots, celery, green or red peppers, cauliflower, cucumber). Your child can dip these for lunch.

MAKES ½ CUP

Orange, Cucumber and Peanut Salad

1 cucumber, scrubbed and thinly sliced
   (not peeled)
1 navel orange, peeled, quartered and
   thinly sliced
1 tablespoon chopped peanuts (add more
   if you like)
1 tablespoon rice vinegar
1 tablespoon Oriental sesame oil
   Salt and pepper

In a plastic container, mix together all of the ingredients. Season with salt and pepper to taste. Cover tightly.

Be sure to include a plastic spoon or fork in the lunch box.

Peanut Rice Faces

Rice cakes (unsalted)
Peanut butter
Sliced banana
Raisins

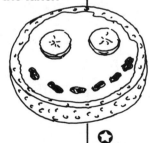

Take a rice cake (you can find them boxed at any market) and spread it with peanut butter. Use 2 slices of banana to shape "eyes" and set them in the peanut butter. Make a smiling mouth with a few raisins. Cover the face with plastic wrap, which will keep it intact in your child's lunch box.

✪

Indian Peanut Dip can also be used for dipping pieces of chicken, sesame pita chips, potato skins, etc.

✪

When you make Peanut Rice Faces, the leftover banana can be sliced and added to plain yogurt and served at breakfast.

SOUPS

VEGETABLE MINESTRONE SOUP
CHICKEN NOODLE SOUP
EGG DROP SOUP
MARC'S FAVORITE
  NOT-TOO-HOT CHILI
CREAM OF TOMATO SOUP
NANA'S BEEF
  AND BARLEY SOUP

Vegetable Minestrone Soup

¼ cup olive oil, or 4 tablespoons unsalted margarine
2 onions, thinly sliced
2 cups sliced carrots
2 cups peeled diced potatoes
3 broccoli florets, cut up
4 zucchini, sliced
2 cups cut-up green beans, or 1 package (10 ounces) frozen green beans
1½ quarts (6 cups) low-sodium chicken broth
1 can (16 ounces) Italian plum tomatoes, drained and cut up
¼ teaspoon celery salt
1 package (10 ounces) frozen spinach
1 can (15 ounces) pinto beans, drained
1 can (15 ounces) red kidney beans, drained
1 cup uncooked macaroni, any size

Heat the oil in a very large pot over moderate heat. The cooking method is easy to remember—add each of the vegetables in turn and cook each for 3 to 4 minutes. Start with the onions and cook until soft. Add the carrots and cook, and then add the potatoes, broccoli, zucchini and green beans in turn.

Add the chicken broth, tomatoes and celery salt. Reduce the heat to low and let the whole concoction cook for 1 hour.

Add the frozen spinach and cook for 10 minutes. Add the beans and macaroni and cook for another 10 minutes. If you find the soup is getting too thick, add 1 cup of water. Let the soup cool before refrigerating.

In the morning, heat 1 serving and put immediately into a thermos.

Chicken Noodle Soup

2½ quarts (10 cups) chicken broth
1 cup dry white wine
4 chicken parts (best is a combination of breasts, legs and thighs; you can include some necks)
4 medium leeks (white part only)
½ cup (1 stick) unsalted butter
2 medium carrots, peeled and finely chopped
3 celery ribs, finely chopped
2 teaspoons coarse (kosher) salt
1 teaspoon black pepper
8 medium mushrooms, wiped clean and thinly sliced
2 cups cooked vermicelli (thin) noodles or alphabet noodles
3 tablespoons chopped parsley
1 tablespoon chopped fresh dill

In a large saucepan, bring the chicken broth and wine to a boil. Add the chicken. Reduce the heat and simmer, uncovered, for 20 minutes. Remove the chicken; place on a dish and let cool. Reserve the poaching liquid.

Annie always reserves half of the Minestrone and freezes it. Weeks later she defrosts it and purees it in the food processor. It becomes a wonderful cream of vegetable soup you can serve for dinner or put into the lunch box.

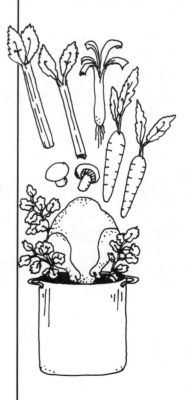

continued

If your child loves Chinese food, you can add other Chinese vegetables, such as bamboo shoots (8 ounces has over 1,200 mg of potassium), Chinese mushrooms, Chinese cabbage, seaweed, snow peas and water chestnuts to the Egg Drop Soup.

Here is another fun treat for the lunch box—one which will make your child the talk of his class. Take a small pair of wooden chopsticks (the disposable paper-wrapped kind you buy at the market). Fold the piece of paper they were wrapped in into a small 1- by ½-inch piece and place between the chopsticks at one end. Wrap a rubber band around the chopsticks at that end. The result is a Chinese tweezer the kids can use to eat the vegetables (or just the tofu) out of the soup.

Trim the leeks and cut lengthwise in half. Wash thoroughly, taking care to remove all of the grit. Dice the leeks.

Melt the butter in a heavy large saucepan over moderately low heat. Add the leeks, carrots, celery, salt and pepper. Cook gently for 5 minutes. Remove from the heat.

Add the chicken poaching liquid and the mushrooms to the vegetables. Simmer, uncovered, over low heat for about 10 minutes. Add the noodles and simmer for another 5 minutes. Remove from the heat.

Remove and discard any skin from the chicken. Pull the meat off the bones; discard the bones. In a food processor, dice the chicken meat by pulsing on and off, making sure not to over-dice. Add the meat to the soup. Stir in the parsley and dill. Simmer for 20 minutes. Remove from the heat and let cool before refrigerating.

You can freeze this soup in individual plastic containers and defrost each the night before. In the morning, heat a portion of soup in the microwave or on the stovetop and pour immediately into a thermos.

Egg Drop Soup

- 2 eggs
- 1 tablespoon cornstarch
- 1½ quarts (6 cups) chicken broth
- ¼ teaspoon minced dill
- ¼ teaspoon sugar
- Pinch of celery salt
- 1 tablespoon soy sauce
- 1 cup tofu

In a small bowl, beat the eggs with 2 teaspoons of water. Set aside.

In another bowl, mix the cornstarch with 3 tablespoons of cold water to form a thick paste.

Bring the chicken broth to a boil in a large pot. Add the dill, sugar, celery salt and soy sauce. Reduce the heat to low and cook for 5 minutes. Add the cornstarch and stir until the soup thickens. While simmering, pour in the eggs, a teaspoonful at a time, stirring constantly. The eggs will separate into shreds. Add the tofu pieces. Remove from heat and let cool before refrigerating.

In the morning, heat a portion in the microwave or on the stovetop and put immediately into a thermos.

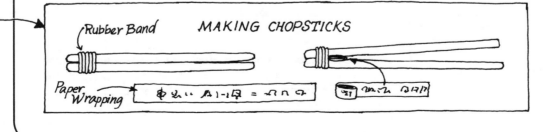

Rubber Band   MAKING CHOPSTICKS

Paper Wrapping

Marc's Favorite Not-Too-Hot Chili

1 pound lean ground beef
1 can (15 ounces) red kidney beans, drained
1 can (15 ounces) pinto beans, drained
1 can (16 ounces) tomatoes
2 tablespoons safflower oil
½ cup chopped green bell pepper
1 cup chopped onion
1 garlic clove, crushed
½ cup chopped parsley
2 teaspoons chili powder
2 tablespoons salt
1½ teaspoons pepper
1½ teaspoons cumin seed

In a large saucepan, sauté the meat over moderate heat for 7 to 10 minutes, until browned. Add the beans and tomatoes (with their liquid). Simmer for 5 minutes.

Meanwhile, in a small skillet, heat the oil over moderate heat. Add the green pepper and sauté for 5 minutes. Add the onion and cook, stirring often, until translucent. Stir in the garlic and parsley.

Pour the mixture into the saucepan with the meat. Stir in the chili powder, salt, pepper and cumin seed. Cook for 10 minutes.

Cover and simmer for 30 minutes.

Uncover and cook for another 30 minutes.

Skim any fat from the top. Refrigerate to store.

In the morning, put a small portion in the microwave to warm. Then place in a thermos, pack a plastic spoon and send off for lunch. If your child loves chili, it will be a warming surprise on a cold winter school day.

Sometimes Marc doesn't feel like having beans. This recipe works just fine without them.

★

If your child likes garlic toast, make some in the morning (cream some butter or margarine with garlic powder or ½ garlic clove, mashed, spread on bread and toast). Wrap in aluminum foil.

★

To wake up cream of chicken soup in the winter (and to add easy protein), just stir 1 tablespoon of peanut butter into a cup of soup, mix well and pour into a thermos.

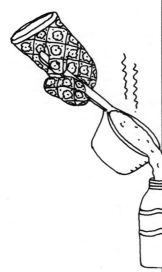

Cream of Tomato Soup

3 to 4 large tomatoes (figure one per
  person)
2 tablespoons butter or margarine
1 scallion, chopped
1 bunch fresh dill, chopped
1 quart (4 cups) chicken broth
1 tablespoon sour cream

Dip the tomatoes into boiling water for 60 seconds. Remove with tongs. Put under cold water and then peel. Chop into small pieces or puree in a food processor.

In a large saucepan, melt the margarine over moderate heat. Add the scallion and sauté without browning. Stir in the tomatoes and dill and cook for 5 to 7 minutes.

Stir in the chicken broth. Cover and simmer for 15 minutes.

Pour the soup into a food processor and puree. Pass the soup through a sieve back into the pot. Warm over low heat. Stir in the sour cream, and heat through but do not boil. Let cool, cover and refrigerate.

In the morning, warm up a portion of the soup and pour into a thermos.

Nana's Beef and Barley Soup

2 to 3 tablespoons vegetable oil or
  shortening
1 pound soup bones
1 pound stewing beef, cut into cubes
½ cup barley
½ teaspoon dried basil
½ teaspoon minced fresh garlic
½ teaspoon dried rosemary
½ teaspoon crumbled bay leaf
½ teaspoon freshly ground pepper
1 to 2 teaspoons salt (or to taste—Nana
  always used more than we do)
1 tablespoon Worcestershire sauce
1 can (16 ounces) tomatoes (if you use the
  whole ones, break them up first)
1 cup sliced celery
1 can (8 ounces) yellow corn, drained, or
  1 package (10 ounces) frozen corn niblets
1 cup string beans, trimmed (fresh limas
  are great, too)

Heat the oil in a large saucepan and brown the bones and beef. Add 2½ quarts water and the barley and simmer for about two hours, skimming off the fat and foam as needed.

Add the seasonings and vegetables and cook for another hour, or until the vegetables are tender. Remove the bones with a slotted spoon and let the soup cool before refrigerating.

In the morning, heat a portion in the microwave or on the stovetop and pour immediately into a thermos.

TREATS/SNACKS

BLOND BROWNIES
JOANNA'S CHOCOLATE CHIP MERINGUE KISSES
LEMON SQUARES
GOLDINE'S BROWNIES
CHEDDAR POPCORN
DATED OATMEAL COOKIES
TOM'S HOMEMADE GRANOLA
NUTTY ORIENTAL MIX
SUPER FUDGE
CURRIED OR CINNAMONED SHREDDED WHEAT
ELLEN'S THUMBPRINT COOKIES
SESAME BARS
POTATO CHIPS
MOM'S MEMORABLE APPLESAUCE
FORTUNE COOKIES
ROASTED PUMPKIN SEEDS
SMOOTHIE

Blond Brownies

1 cup (2 sticks) butter, at room temperature
1 cup all-purpose flour
1 cup granulated sugar
1 cup packed brown sugar
1 tablespoon baking powder
2 eggs
Pinch of salt
½ cup coarsely chopped walnuts
4 ounces (¼ cup) chocolate bits or
mini-chips
Powdered sugar, for dusting the tops

Preheat the oven to 375 degrees. Butter a 9- x 12-inch glass baking dish or a jelly roll pan.

In the bowl of an electric mixer, cream together the butter, flour and granulated sugar until fluffy. Add the brown sugar, baking powder, eggs and salt, and beat until well mixed. Fold in the walnuts by hand.

Spread the batter in the prepared pan. Sprinkle on the chocolate bits.

Bake for 15 minutes. Reduce the heat to 350 degrees and bake for another 15 minutes. To test for doneness, the toothpick should not come out clean—these brownies should be chewy.

Sift the powdered sugar over the top while they are still warm. Cut into squares. Store covered.

MAKES ABOUT 16 BROWNIES

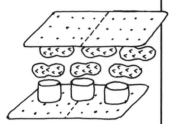

★

Donnie Smith's kids' favorite lunch-box treats were graham cracker sandwiches filled with peanut butter and marshmallow whip. "I figured all that protein in the peanut butter made up for the sugar in the marshmallows," says Donnie. Whether it did or not, the Smith graham cracker sandwiches still bring fond memories to the now grown kids.

Joanna's Chocolate Chip Meringue Kisses

4 egg whites, at room temperature
⅛ teaspoon salt
¼ teaspoon cream of tartar
1 cup granulated sugar
1 teaspoon vanilla extract
1 cup mini chocolate chips

Preheat the oven to 300 degrees. Spray a cookie sheet with vegetable spray.

In the mixing bowl of an electric mixer, beat the egg whites with the salt and cream of tartar. Begin beating on low and gradually increase the speed to high. Beat until soft peaks form.

Gradually add the sugar and continue beating. Add the vanilla and beat until the peaks are stiff. Fold in the chocolate chips by hand.

Drop teaspoonfuls of the mixture onto the prepared baking sheet. Bake for 25 minutes. Turn off the heat and allow the kisses to cool in the oven for about 10 minutes. (You may need to repeat the process, depending on the size of your cookie sheet and kisses.)

Store the kisses airtight in a tin. Send to school in plastic sandwich bags.

Lemon Squares

Adapted from Laurie Burrows Grad in her book, Make It Easy in Your Kitchen, *J. P. Tarcher, Inc., 1982.*

1 cup plus 2 tablespoons all-purpose flour
6 tablespoons (¾ stick) unsalted butter, softened
¼ cup powdered sugar
1½ ounces cream cheese, softened
1 cup sugar
2 eggs, lightly beaten
3 tablespoons fresh lemon juice
1 teaspoon finely minced lemon rind
½ teaspoon baking powder
Powdered sugar for garnishing

Preheat the oven to 350 degrees. Generously butter an 8-inch square baking pan and lightly dust with flour.

In a large mixing bowl with an electric mixer, combine 1 cup flour, the butter, ¼ cup powdered sugar and the cream cheese and beat until crumbly.

Press the dough into the prepared baking pan and bake for 20 minutes. In the meantime, combine the 2 tablespoons flour, sugar, eggs, lemon juice, lemon rind and baking powder and beat until smooth. Spread the mixture over the baked layer and return to the oven for another 25 minutes.

Remove from the oven and cool in the pan for about 10 minutes. Then, while still warm, run a knife around the outer edge and cut into bars. Wrap each bar in-dividually in plastic wrap and freeze. In the morning, take out a bar, unwrap, and place in a plastic bag. It will defrost by lunchtime.

MAKES ABOUT 16 SQUARES

Goldine's Brownies

1 cup (2 sticks) butter or margarine
2 squares (2 ounces) unsweetened chocolate
1 cup granulated sugar
⅔ cup self-rising flour
1 teaspoon vanilla extract
2 eggs
¾ cup pecan pieces
Powdered sugar

Preheat the oven to 350 degrees. Butter the bottom and sides of an 8-inch square pan.

In a saucepan, melt the butter with the chocolate over low heat. Remove from the heat.

Stir in the granulated sugar, flour and vanilla. Mix well. Beat in the eggs. Stir in the pecans.

Spread the batter in the prepared pan and smooth the top. Bake for about 30 minutes, or until a toothpick inserted in the center comes out clean. Let cool in the pan on a wire rack.

Sprinkle the top with the powdered sugar and cut into squares. Store covered.

MAKES ABOUT 16 BROWNIES

✪

Why not double these recipes? Bake for the same amount of time in two 8-inch square pans or one 19- x 13- x 2-inch pan. You'll then have lots of extras in your freezer for lunches or after-dinner treats.

You can make the cheese popcorn with other kinds of cheeses. You can also make it the night before. Annie makes popcorn at night if the family is watching a movie. She then takes the leftover popcorn, turns it into cheese popcorn and packs it in the lunch box the next morning.

Cheddar Popcorn

Definitely not just a kid's food, popcorn has recently pushed its way onto the gourmet shelves with its many variations. What used to be a popular variation on a theme, caramel popcorn, has now been joined by Jalapeño Cheese Popcorn, Bacon and Cheese Popcorn, Sour Cream and Onion Popcorn, Butter Pecan Popcorn, Cinnamon-Spice Popcorn, Tangerine Popcorn and the like. Plain popcorn—unbuttered and unsalted—is a good food. It has only 25 calories per cup and traces of protein, carbohydrate, calcium and phosphorus. It is easy to pack in a plastic baggie and is a good alternative surprise. If you are a parent, or just an American, we're pretty sure you know how to make popcorn. But here's a recipe for our favorite—Cheddar Cheese Popcorn.

4 to 6 cups popped popcorn
½ cup (1 stick) margarine, at room
temperature
½ cup grated cheddar cheese
½ teaspoon salt

Make the popcorn as you normally do; place in a plastic bag and seal.

In the morning, in a small bowl, mix together the margarine, cheese and salt. Melt on the stovetop or in a microwave. Pour over the popcorn and let cool for a few minutes.

Place a portion in a plastic bag and send off in the lunch box.

Dated Oatmeal Cookies

1½ **cups whole wheat flour**
3 **tablespoons wheat germ**
1 **teaspoon baking soda**
1 **teaspoon cinnamon**
½ **teaspoon salt**
¼ **teaspoon ground nutmeg**
2 **eggs**
¾ **cup packed brown sugar**
¼ **cup orange honey**
1 **cup (2 sticks) margarine, at room**
temperature
3 **cups rolled oats**
1 **cup chopped dates**

Preheat the oven to 350 degrees. Lightly butter a baking sheet.

In a bowl, combine the flour, wheat germ, baking soda, cinnamon, salt and nutmeg. Set aside.

In a food processor, mix together the eggs, brown sugar, honey and margarine until smooth. Stir in the flour mixture to make a moist dough. Add the oats and dates and mix well.

Drop the cookies by the teaspoonful onto the prepared baking sheet, spacing them about 2 inches apart. Bake for 8 to 10 minutes, or until golden. Cool on a wire rack. Store in a covered cookie jar or tin.

Tom's Homemade Granola

Meredith's husband, Tom, has been making this granola since the family lived in California. Whenever someone asks Tom to send in his favorite recipe, whether it's a main dish or a dessert, he automatically sends the granola. And at the Brokaw household, all visitors, especially the girls' friends, expect to find a full granola jar in the kitchen. So here's the "famous recipe" that has been packed in all Brokaw lunch boxes (and in hikers' backpacks as well).

    4 cups old-fashioned oats
    1 cup shredded coconut
    ⅓ cup sesame seeds
    1 cup wheat germ
    ½ cup safflower oil
    ½ cup honey
    3 cups mixed nuts, such as slivered
        almonds, walnuts and pine nuts
    2 to 3 cups dried fruits (apples, pears,
        cherries, apricots, raisins), diced

Preheat the oven to 300 degrees.

Combine the oats, coconut, sesame seeds and wheat germ in a large heatproof bowl.

In a medium saucepan, warm the oil and honey until bubbly.

Pour the warm honey and oil mixture onto the oat mixture and stir to coat. Add the nuts.

Spread the entire mixture over shallow baking pans.

Bake, stirring frequently, for about 25 minutes, or until golden brown.

Remove from oven and let cool. Stir in the dried fruits. That's it!

Store in an airtight container.

Nutty Oriental Mix

    1¼ cups raw cashews or peanuts
    ¾ cup unsalted soy nuts
    1 cup raw sunflower seeds, unhulled
        pumpkin seeds or a mixture of the two
    4 teaspoons safflower or corn oil
    2 teaspoons Oriental sesame oil, or
        2 tablespoons peanut oil
    2 teaspoons soy sauce
    ¾ teaspoon sugar
    ½ teaspoon salt
    ¼ teaspoon ground ginger
    ⅛ teaspoon garlic powder

Preheat the oven to 300 degrees. Oil a baking sheet (or spray with a vegetable spray).

In a large bowl, combine the nuts and seeds. Pour the oil and all of the seasonings into a jar, cover with a lid and shake to mix. Pour over the nut and seed mixture. Toss to coat.

Spread the mixture evenly on the prepared baking sheet. Bake for 20 minutes, or until the nuts are lightly toasted. Cool. Refrigerate in covered jars or cans.

✿

If you make the Oriental Mix using salted nuts, omit the salt in the recipe.

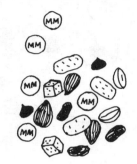

★

Meredith Petrin's mom mixes croutons, small pretzels, dried fruit, raisins and whatever nuts she has in the house for her own version of trail mix. "Sometimes," she whispers, "I mix in some M&Ms."

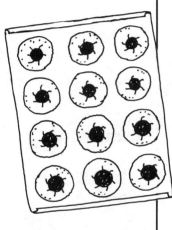

★

If the Super Fudge is too sweet for your liking, use ½ cup plus 1 tablespoon honey instead of ¾ cup.

Super Fudge

 2 squares (2 ounces) unsweetened chocolate, coarsely chopped
1 cup peanut butter
¾ cup honey
½ cup sesame seeds
½ sunflower seeds
¼ cup shredded coconut

Butter an 8-inch square pan or dish. In a nonstick saucepan, melt together the chocolate, peanut butter and honey over moderately low heat.

In a separate bowl, combine the sesame seeds, sunflower seeds and coconut. Stir into the chocolate mixture.

Press the mixture into the prepared pan. Let cool to harden.

Cut into squares.

MAKES ABOUT 16 SQUARES

Curried or Cinnamoned Shredded Wheat

6 tablespoons (¾ stick) butter or margarine
½ teaspoon curry powder or ground cinnamon
¼ teaspoon onion salt
⅛ teaspoon ground ginger (or nutmeg if you are using cinnamon)
3 cups spoon-size Shredded Wheat

Melt the butter in a large skillet over moderate heat. Stir in the seasonings. Add the Shredded Wheat and toss to coat.

Cook, stirring frequently, for about 5 minutes. Drain on paper towels.

Refrigerate for 5 to 10 minutes, then pack as needed in a plastic bag in the lunch box.

Ellen's Thumbprint Cookies

These are a big item on the school trading tray—which means Ellen doubles the recipe every time.

 1 cup (2 sticks) butter, at room temperature
½ cup sugar
2 cups all-purpose flour
2 egg yolks
1 teaspoon almond or vanilla extract
Jelly or peanut butter

Preheat the oven to 350 degrees. Grease a cookie sheet.

In a bowl, mix together all of the ingredients except for the jelly or peanut butter.

Roll out the dough to ½-inch thickness on a floured surface. Cut into 1-inch squares. Press your child's thumb on each and fill the depression with jelly or peanut butter.

Bake on a cookie sheet for 12 minutes, or until lightly browned. Cool on a wire rack, and store in a covered tin.

MAKES 8 TO 12 COOKIES

✿

You can also add peanuts, sunflower seeds, raisins or any other dried fruits or nuts to the Shredded Wheat.

Sesame Bars

This recipe is fun for the kids to make and the bars will keep well if stored in a covered container.

3 cups sesame seeds
1 cup unsweetened shredded coconut
2 tablespoons soft peanut butter
2 tablespoons honey
½ teaspoon salt
¼ teaspoon vanilla extract

Preheat the oven to 250 degrees. Butter a baking sheet or large baking pan.

Mix together all of the ingredients and keep working the mixture—it will seem dry at first, but don't add water or any liquids to it.

Empty the bowl onto the prepared pan and press the mixture into it. Bake for about 30 to 45 minutes, or until browned. Watch to make sure it doesn't burn. Let cool and cut into bars.

MAKES ABOUT 8 BARS

Potato Chips

These delicious chips contain no salt or fat.

4 baking potatoes
4 cups ice cold water

Very thinly slice the potatoes in a food processor. Put the slices in ice water and refrigerate for about 30 minutes (the water will prevent the potatoes from turning brown).

Preheat the oven to 450 degrees.

Drain the potatoes and dry completely with paper towels.

Spread enough of the chips on a nonstick baking sheet to cover the bottom without overlapping. Bake for about 5 minutes, until brown on one side. Turn over with tongs and bake for 5 minutes more.

Take out and let cool on a plate. Repeat the procedure until all of the chips have been baked.

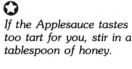

Mom's Memorable Applesauce

This recipe is easy to make, and it tastes so wonderful that you may never choose to buy applesauce in jars again! This is especially simple to make if you have a crock pot left over from the 70s—just make it the night before.

8 to 10 cored, peeled and quartered Pippin or Rome Beauty apples (or any good baking apple)
1 teaspoon fresh lemon juice
Dash of ground cinammon

Place the apples in the crock pot. Add the lemon juice and cinnamon. Turn the crock pot on low. Leave it on all night (or all day), about 8 hours. That's it.

MAKES 4 TO 5 CUPS

☆
For a special and different treat, try making potato chips using sweet potatoes.

☆
If the Applesauce tastes too tart for you, stir in a tablespoon of honey.

HONEY

Of all nuts and seeds, the highest and most complete protein is found in pumpkin seeds. Cheese and sesame seeds are also good sources of protein and add flavor to this recipe.

Fortune Cookies

½ cup sugar
2 egg whites
Pinch of salt
¼ cup melted margarine
¼ cup all-purpose flour
¼ teaspoon vanilla extract

Prepare 15 personal "fortunes" for your child on 2 ½- x ½-inch slips of paper.

Preheat the oven to 350 degrees. Butter a baking sheet.

In a mixing bowl, stir the sugar into the egg whites. Add the salt. When the sugar is fully dissolved, add the margarine, flour, and vanilla and beat with a mixer until smooth.

Drop the batter, 1 teaspoonful at a time, on the prepared baking pan, spacing them 2 inches apart. Bake for 5 minutes, or until the edges are browned.

Transfer the cookies to a cutting board. While still warm, put one "fortune" across the center of each circle and fold each cookie over to form a semicircle. Fold the semicircles over the edge of a bowl to shape them. Let cool in place.

You will have to work fast because the cookies are flexible only when they are warm. If necessary, return any "unfortuned" cookies to the oven for a minute or so to warm up and become pliable again.

MAKES 15 COOKIES

Roasted Pumpkin Seeds

2 cups hulled raw pumpkin seeds
¼ cup unhulled sesame seeds
2 tablespoons grated Parmesan or romano cheese
1 tablespoon butter or safflower margarine, melted
1 tablespoon Worcestershire sauce
Salt

Preheat the oven to 375 degrees.

Combine all of the ingredients. Season to taste with salt. Spread out the mixture on a baking sheet.

Bake, stirring frequently, until lightly toasted. Let cool.

To store, fill jars or cans, cover and refrigerate.

Smoothie

1 egg
⅓ cup milk
¼ cup fresh berries, such as strawberries, raspberries, blueberries or mixture

Combine all of the ingredients in a blender or food processor. Process for 1 minute.

Pour into a chilled thermos as this must be kept cool.

It tastes great and kids will never know there is an egg in it!

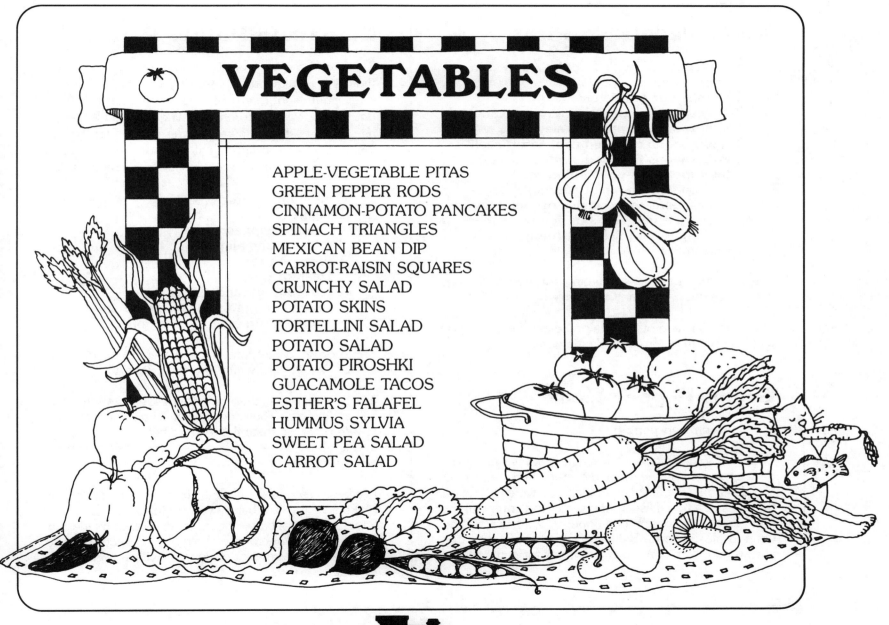

VEGETABLES

APPLE-VEGETABLE PITAS
GREEN PEPPER RODS
CINNAMON-POTATO PANCAKES
SPINACH TRIANGLES
MEXICAN BEAN DIP
CARROT-RAISIN SQUARES
CRUNCHY SALAD
POTATO SKINS
TORTELLINI SALAD
POTATO SALAD
POTATO PIROSHKI
GUACAMOLE TACOS
ESTHER'S FALAFEL
HUMMUS SYLVIA
SWEET PEA SALAD
CARROT SALAD

★
Keep handy any fresh vegetables, cut up and stored in a bowl of ice water. When ready to pack your child's lunch box, drain the vegetables and wrap in plastic. The vegetables can be cut in unusual shapes, too. Peel a carrot using a peeler, then soak in cold water to keep carrot "curls" fresh.

Apple-Vegetable Pitas

¼ cup chopped peeled apples (dipped in lemon juice)
¼ chopped or grated carrot
3 tablespoons chopped celery (optional)
1 tablespoon chopped parsley
3 tablespoons chopped cooked broccoli
2 tablespoons chopped seeded cucumber
1 tablespoon chopped onion
3 tablespoons chopped zucchini
2 tablespoons mayonnaise or plain yogurt (more if you like, but you want the filling to be thick, not runny)
1 pita bread

In a bowl, mix together everything but the bread. (You can substitute or add any vegetables.)

Slice open one end of the pita bread and fill the pocket with the mixture. Wrap in plastic wrap.

Green Pepper Rods

1 green bell pepper

You want something easy? Just take a well-washed green bell pepper, cut off the top and bottom, and stand it up. Cut down on four sides as though you were cutting off the sides of a box. Discard the seeds and core. Cut the four pieces into rods. When done, take a few rods and wrap in plastic wrap. Refrigerate the others—you can always add them to another lunch box for nutrition and crunch.

Cinnamon-Potato Pancakes

This recipe makes a lot of pancakes and it takes a little time. We wouldn't advise making it in the morning, or on Sunday night (pancakes really aren't terrific after a day or so). We do recommend making the pancakes for dinner one evening and keeping the leftovers for the kids' lunches. The next morning all you have to do is warm them up in the toaster oven and wrap in aluminum foil.

6 medium potatoes, peeled
1 egg
1 onion, chopped
3 tablespoons all-purpose flour
1 teaspoon salt
Dash of pepper
¼ teaspoon ground cinnamon
Butter, margarine or oil, for frying (enough to keep the pan oiled)

Shred or grind the potatoes in a blender or food processor. Wash with water and then drain well.

In a bowl, mix together the potatoes, egg, onion, flour, salt and pepper. Then add the cinnamon (you may want to add more, so taste the mixture before and after you add it. Don't be too generous—a little bit of cinnamon goes a long way).

In a large heavy skillet, melt the butter over medium heat. Make sure it is hot before you begin to fry. Use about 2 tablespoons of batter for each pancake. Cook the pancakes until golden brown on both sides. As each is ready, remove to a warm platter covered with a paper towel to drain.

Serve the pancakes with plain yogurt, applesauce or sour cream. Refrigerate the leftovers.

MAKES 12 MEDIUM PANCAKES

Spinach Triangles

> 1 tablespoon butter
> ½ cup chopped onion
> 3 scallions, trimmed and minced
> ¼ cup minced parsley
> 1¼ teaspoons dried dill, crushed
> ¼ teaspoon salt
> 2 eggs
> 1 pound spinach, chopped, steamed and squeezed dry, or 1 package (10 ounces) frozen chopped spinach, thawed and squeezed dry
> 8 ounces feta (or ricotta) cheese, crumbled
> ⅓ cup grated Parmesan cheese
>   Poppin' Fresh crescent dough

Preheat the oven to 350 degrees.

In a small skillet, melt the butter over moderate heat. Add the onions and scallions and sauté until soft. Add the parsley, dill and salt. Cook, stirring, until heated through.

In a large bowl, beat the eggs. Stir in the sautéed onion-herb mixture. Sprinkle in the spinach and cheeses and mix well. Prepare the pastry dough, roll out and fill. Fold into turnover-shaped wedges (triangles) and bake for 8 to 12 minutes, checking to make sure the sides aren't getting too brown. Store wrapped in the refrigerator or freeze.

MAKES 12

Mexican Bean Dip

> ½ cup (1 stick) butter or margarine
> 1 onion, chopped
> 1 can (8 ounces) green chiles, drained and diced
> 1 can (15 ounces) refried beans
> 2 cups grated cheddar cheese

In a saucepan, melt the butter over moderate heat. Add the onion and chiles and sauté for 5 to 10 minutes. Add the beans and cook until a thick bean paste is formed.

In the morning, warm up in the microwave or toaster oven, add the cheese and send in a plastic container with tortilla chips (or our homemade potato chips, page 71).

Carrot-Raisin Squares

> 1 cup grated carrots
> 3 tablespoons mayonnaise
> ½ cup chopped unsalted nuts (peanuts or walnuts are best)
> 1 tablespoon fresh lemon juice
> ¼ teaspoon salt
>   Drop of Worcestershire sauce
> 2 to 4 slices cinnamon-raisin bread

In a bowl, mix all of the ingredients except the bread. Cover and chill for as long as you can (but even 5 or 10 minutes will do).

Toast the slices of cinnamon-raisin bread (you can buy it at any market). Spread the carrot mixture on the bread. Cover. Cut each sandwich into 4 squares and wrap well.

Make the Mexican Bean Dip with green beans instead of refried beans. When cooked, put the mixture in the food processor and beat to form a smooth dip.

There are so many possible fillings for a potato skin. First establish which are your child's favorite fillings of any sort—chances are you can stuff a potato skin with them. Some suggestions:

cheddar cheese (broiled in toaster oven)
cottage cheese and crumbled bacon
mashed avocado or guacamole salad (page 78)
salsa
cream cheese and chives
tuna or salmon salad
dab of sour cream

Crunchy Salad

1 onion, thinly sliced
2 tablespoons fresh lemon juice
2 tablespoons fresh lime juice
   Pinch of grated lemon zest
¼ teaspoon salt
¾ cup olive oil
1¾ pounds jicama, peeled and julienned, or
   1 bunch celery, cut up (or any other sliced vegetable)
1 head butter lettuce

Cover the onion with lightly salted cold water and set aside to soak for 2 hours.

To make a vinaigrette, blend the lemon and lime juices, lemon zest and salt in a small bowl. While whisking, pour in the oil in a thin stream.

Drain the onion and pat dry. Place in a larger bowl. Add the jicama and toss with the vinaigrette. Send in a covered container. Remember the fork!

Potato Skins

3 baking potatoes
   A filling of your choice

Preheat the oven (or toaster oven) to 400 degrees.

Wash the potatoes well (scrub with a vegetable brush). Wrap each in aluminum foil and place on the rack in the middle of the oven. Prick each potato with a fork. Bake for 1 hour (test with a fork to see if the potato is soft). Remove from the oven and let cool. Leave the oven on.

Cut each potato in half and scoop out the filling (reserve and make mashed potatoes for dinner). Cut each half lengthwise in half. Return to the oven and bake for another 30 minutes, or until crisp. Let cool.

Wrap the potatoes in plastic wrap and refrigerate. In the morning, take out 2 to 4 skins and fill. Warm in the oven. Wrap in aluminum foil and put in the lunch box.

Tortellini Salad

2 cups uncooked tortellini, filled with cheese or spinach
½ green bell pepper, chopped
½ red bell pepper, chopped
   Carrots, tomatoes, and/or any other vegetables of your choice
¼ cup olive oil
1 teaspoon white wine vinegar or lemon juice
½ teaspoon Dijon mustard
1 tablespoon chopped fresh basil, or
   ½ teaspoon dried basil leaves

In a large pot, cook the pasta in boiling water until al dente—don't overcook. Drain well and place in a large bowl. Add the green and red bell peppers and any other fresh vegetables to the tortellini.

In a jar, mix together the remaining ingredients to make a light vinaigrette sauce. Cover and shake well.

Pour over the pasta. This dish can be eaten at room temperature. Store covered in the refrigerator.

Potato Salad

12 ounces red potatoes
1 hard-cooked egg, chopped
½ small onion, chopped
1 tablespoon chopped parsley
2 tablespoons chopped tomato
2 tablespoons chopped pickles (optional)
1½ tablespoons any type of vinegar
3 tablespoons olive oil
Pinch of salt
Pinch of pepper

In a saucepan, place the potatoes in salted water to cover and bring to a boil. Cover and cook for 10 minutes. Remove from the heat and let stand, covered, for 15 minutes more (this lets them cook a little longer). Drain well.

Cut the potatoes into bite-size pieces. Place in a large bowl. Add the egg, onion, parsley, tomato and pickles.

In a jar, combine the vinegar, oil, salt and pepper. Cover and shake well. Pour over the potato salad and toss gently to coat. Cover and refrigerate.

Potato Piroshki

This recipe makes 8 crescents, but you can either freeze or refrigerate the excess for up to a week.

8 small potatoes, peeled
4 tablespoons butter
1 cup chopped onion
1 package Poppin' Fresh crescent dough

Preheat the oven to 325 degrees.

Boil the potatoes; drain well. Add 2 tablespoons of the butter and mash the potatoes by hand.

In a skillet, melt the remaining 2 tablespoons butter over moderate heat. Add the onions and sauté until lightly browned. Add to the potatoes.

Remove the dough from the can and unroll the triangles on a cutting board. With a rolling pin, flatten each triangle of dough a little more. Place a scoop of the potato filling on each of the triangles. Now take the 3 ends and fold over, making sure to seal the piroshki.

Put all the piroshki on a buttered baking sheet. Bake until the dough is brown, about 15 minutes. Let cool and refrigerate or freeze.

In the morning, take out a piroshki and warm it in the toaster oven. Wrap in foil and pop it in the lunch box.

For variety, add 1 tablespoon white tuna to the potato salad.

Paul Herman and his son Andrew came up with an alternative to potato chips—pita sesame chips. Paul starts by separating the pitas and dividing each circle into quarters. He spreads the insides with margarine and sprinkles on sesame seeds. He puts the chips in the toaster oven until they are lightly brown. Andrew loves to dip them in peanut sauce or guacamole.

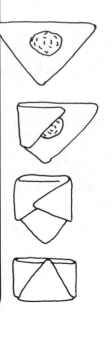

Guacamole Tacos

Tacos have always been favorites for evening meals and lunchtime treats on weekends, but they also wrap well and make a special and nutritious treat for your child's lunch box. If your child doesn't like guacamole, leave it out. The taco is perfectly delicious without it.

First make the guacamole, leaving the avocado pit in the mixture to keep it from turning brown.

Guacamole:

> 1 ripe avocado, peeled and pitted
> (reserve the pit)
> ½ onion, chopped
> 2 tablespoons fresh lemon juice
> ½ tomato, minced
> Pinch of garlic salt
> 1 teaspoon store-bought salsa

> 8 ounces lean ground beef, browned
> Taco shells
> Shredded lettuce
> 2 slices tomato, chopped
> 2 tablespoons shredded cheddar cheese
> Guacamole

Mix together all the ingredients for the guacamole, either by hand or in a blender or food processor. Place the avocado pit in the mixture. Cover and refrigerate.

When preparing the guacamole tacos, you can brown the hamburger meat ahead of time and keep it covered in the refrigerator until you are read to use it. Fill the taco shell with the ground meat, a pinch of shredded lettuce, some chopped tomato, cheddar cheese and 1 tablespoon or so of guacamole. If there is room, add another tablespoon of guacamole (but don't fill the taco too high).

Esther's Falafel

> 1 can (19 ounces) chick-peas, drained
> ½ cup chopped parsley
> ½ cup canned tahini (sesame seed paste)
> 2 to 3 garlic cloves, crushed
> 1 egg, beaten with 1 tablespoon water
> 1 teaspoon ground coriander
> 1 teaspoon ground cumin
> ½ cup chopped onion
> 1 cup fine dry bread crumbs
> ½ teaspoon baking powder
> Salt
> Pinch of cayenne pepper
> 1 teaspoon Worcestershire sauce
> 3 cups vegetable oil
> Pita bread
> Chopped lettuce and tomato
> 1 dill pickle, sliced

Tahini Sauce

> 1 cup low-fat plain yogurt
> ½ cup canned tahini (sesame seed paste)
> Pinch of ground coriander

✪
We have made our Tahini Sauce thicker than usual so it won't run when poured into the pita and make the sandwich soft.

✪
If your child is adventurous and likes spicy food, you can double up on the spices in the Falafel (try using ¼ teaspoon of cayenne pepper rather than just a pinch).

In a food processor, puree the chick-peas with the parsley, pulsing on and off. Don't overprocess. Transfer to a large mixing bowl. Add the tahini paste and the garlic and mix well. Combine the egg-water mixture, spices, onion, bread crumbs, baking powder, salt, cayenne pepper and Worcestershire. Add to the chick-peas and parsley mixture and mix well with a wooden spoon.

Fill a deep, heavy saucepan with the oil and heat until very hot. Now wet your hands. Take a tablespoon of the falafel mixture and mold in your hands into a small ball. Drop into the saucepan. Keep this up until the pot is full of falafel balls, making sure not to crowd them. Each ball should have enough oil around it so it can brown on all sides. Watch to make sure they don't burn. When browned, take out and let drain on a paper towel. Repeat the procedure with the rest of the falafel batter.

To make the Tahini Sauce, merely combine the yogurt, tahini and coriander in a small mixing bowl. You can make this the night before, too, and keep it refrigerated for 3 to 4 days.

When the falafel balls are done and drained, refrigerate covered. In the morning, take a pita bread and cut about ½ inch off the top. This creates a pocket. Fill with chopped lettuce, tomatoes, pickles, and two to three falafel balls. Wrap in aluminum foil. Fill a small plastic container half way full with the falafel sauce. When your child is ready to eat the "falafel sandwich," he can dip it into the sauce or pour some into the pita.

Hummus Sylvia

1½ cups drained canned chick-peas
3 garlic cloves
½ teaspoon salt
Dash of tamari
Juice of 2 lemons
¾ cup tahini (sesame seed paste)
¼ cup packed minced parsley
¼ cup minced scallions
Black pepper
Dash of cayenne pepper

In the food processor, mash the chick-peas into a thick paste. Incorporate all of the remaining ingredients. Chill. Taste and correct the seasoning if necessary.

★

If your kid has a passion for sprouts, you can grow your own. Here's how Meredith grows hers:

Wet three tablespoons of alfalfa seeds with water in a 1-quart Mason jar. Drain off the excess water. Cover the opening with cheesecloth and secure with a rubber band. Lay the jar on its side in a dark space (under your kitchen sink is a good place). Rinse and drain daily for 3 days, then bring out to expose the seeds to light. The sprouts will "green up" within a day for delicious eating.

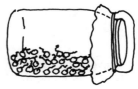

✪

To serve the hummus as a dip, use cut vegetables; fill a pita with the hummus or combine chopped vegetables with the hummus to use as a spread or filling.

When Esther Ancoli makes Sweet Pea Salad in the hot summers of New York, she uses yogurt instead of mayonnaise. It's not that she doesn't like mayonnaise—as a matter of fact, as a bacteriologist, she believes it has gotten a bad rap (it will not spoil in 3 to 4 hours unless it sits outside under a very hot sun). It's just that Grandma Essie prefers the taste of yogurt!

★

If you have leftover cooked carrots, put them into the food processor and add peanuts (2 tablespoons peanuts for 2 cups of carrots), a dab of butter, a tablespoon of sour cream and a pinch each of cinnamon and ginger. Warm in the microwave, place in a plastic dish, cover and send to school.

Sweet Pea Salad

4 cups shelled fresh peas, cooked
1½ cups fresh corn kernels, cooked
½ cup minced scallions
1 cup sour cream
3 tablespoons mayonnaise
¼ cup fresh lemon juice
Pinch of salt and pepper
Chopped peanuts

Place the peas and corn in a bowl and add the scallions, sour cream, mayonnaise, lemon juice and salt and pepper. Cover and chill overnight. In the morning, place a portion in a plastic container, sprinkle on the nuts, cover and pack for lunch.

Carrot Salad

This recipe should be prepared a day ahead of time— letting it marinate makes the salad taste much better.

¾ cup mayonnaise
2 tablespoons vinegar
4 medium carrots, peeled and julienned

Mix the mayonnaise and vinegar together in a small bowl. Place the carrots in a shallow bowl and spoon on the mayonnaise mixture to coat the carrots. Cover and refrigerate overnight.

In the morning, put a portion into a plastic container, cover and send off with a plastic spoon.

A MONTH OF LUNCHES

The following is a sample selection of menus, each of which is a good combination of nutritious foods. This "month of lunches" doesn't mean you must make these menus for a month. Instead, keep in mind that any of these work well on any given day, but make life easy on yourself—serve the foods you cook or bake in the beginning of the week again during the week. Just use your imagination to surprise your child with an interesting "variation on the theme" (peanut bread on Monday can be cut into a different shape on Wednesday and spread with a strawberry butter).

A MONTH OF LUNCHES

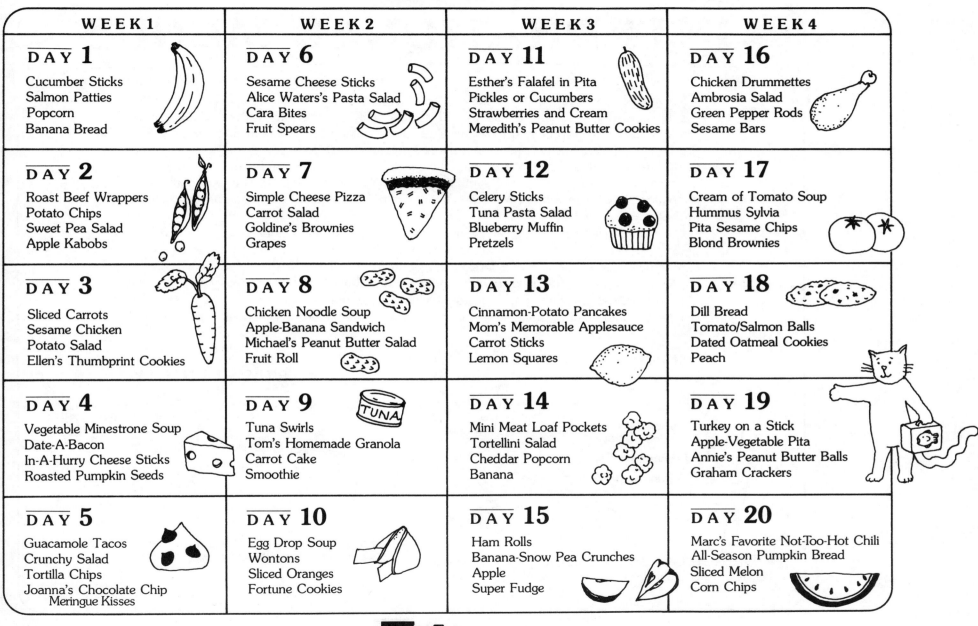

WEEK 1	WEEK 2	WEEK 3	WEEK 4
DAY 1 Cucumber Sticks Salmon Patties Popcorn Banana Bread	**DAY 6** Sesame Cheese Sticks Alice Waters's Pasta Salad Cara Bites Fruit Spears	**DAY 11** Esther's Falafel in Pita Pickles or Cucumbers Strawberries and Cream Meredith's Peanut Butter Cookies	**DAY 16** Chicken Drummettes Ambrosia Salad Green Pepper Rods Sesame Bars
DAY 2 Roast Beef Wrappers Potato Chips Sweet Pea Salad Apple Kabobs	**DAY 7** Simple Cheese Pizza Carrot Salad Goldine's Brownies Grapes	**DAY 12** Celery Sticks Tuna Pasta Salad Blueberry Muffin Pretzels	**DAY 17** Cream of Tomato Soup Hummus Sylvia Pita Sesame Chips Blond Brownies
DAY 3 Sliced Carrots Sesame Chicken Potato Salad Ellen's Thumbprint Cookies	**DAY 8** Chicken Noodle Soup Apple-Banana Sandwich Michael's Peanut Butter Salad Fruit Roll	**DAY 13** Cinnamon-Potato Pancakes Mom's Memorable Applesauce Carrot Sticks Lemon Squares	**DAY 18** Dill Bread Tomato/Salmon Balls Dated Oatmeal Cookies Peach
DAY 4 Vegetable Minestrone Soup Date-A-Bacon In-A-Hurry Cheese Sticks Roasted Pumpkin Seeds	**DAY 9** Tuna Swirls Tom's Homemade Granola Carrot Cake Smoothie	**DAY 14** Mini Meat Loaf Pockets Tortellini Salad Cheddar Popcorn Banana	**DAY 19** Turkey on a Stick Apple-Vegetable Pita Annie's Peanut Butter Balls Graham Crackers
DAY 5 Guacamole Tacos Crunchy Salad Tortilla Chips Joanna's Chocolate Chip Meringue Kisses	**DAY 10** Egg Drop Soup Wontons Sliced Oranges Fortune Cookies	**DAY 15** Ham Rolls Banana-Snow Pea Crunches Apple Super Fudge	**DAY 20** Marc's Favorite Not-Too-Hot Chili All-Season Pumpkin Bread Sliced Melon Corn Chips

INTERNATIONAL MENUS

To break up the lunch box routine, make one day a month (or one day a week) "International Day." Let your child choose his "nationality" for that day at the beginning of the week. You can plan the menu together. You can also shop for accessories together—a little flag or flag sticker (available at most stationery/party stores), foreign money, postcards from the different countries (the pictures teach the kids about the country, and you can send a secret message on the back), a special symbol (for example, for an Oriental Day you could pack chopsticks or a paper fan, for Mexican Day you can pack a "peso" coin), and always napkins in that country's colors.

For an added learning treat, teach your child a few words in that language (you can find inexpensive, pocket-size foreign dictionaries at any bookstore). She will feel so proud when she can actually say something in a foreign tongue in front of her peers!

This can become a fun-filled tradition—you will find that your child will look forward to the planning, the designing, the packing and the eating of his international lunch. And when you've done a few of these days, save the recipes and make an international recipe book with your child.

ORIENTAL DAY

Chicken Drummettes or
Chinese Chicken Salad Sandwich
Peanut Rice Faces
Fortune Cookies

Include chopsticks (made into tweezers, see page 62); a paper fan; tiny paper umbrellas.

RUSSIAN DAY

Potato Piroshki
Mini Meat Loaf Pockets
Strawberries and Cream

Look up a couple of words in a Russian dictionary and write them on a postcard or piece of paper.

AMERICAN DAY

Peanut Butter and Jelly Sandwich

Chocolate Chip Cookies or Brownies

Mom's Memorable Applesauce

Malted Milk or Chocolate Milk

Include paper flags; red, white and blue napkin; streamer left over from the Fourth of July; any appropriate stickers. If you have any small souvenirs (the Statue of Liberty, model space rockets), include them, too.

GREEK DAY

Spinach Triangles (a form of spanakopita)

Olives

Dated Oatmeal Cookies

The Greek flag is a pretty design that is easy to draw on napkins or on a note to your child. You can substitute some Olympic paraphernalia (explain to your child that the Olympics were born in Greece).

SWISS DAY

Any sandwich cut with a cross cookie cutter (the Swiss flag has a cross in the center)

In-A-Hurry Cheese Sticks

Any of our chocolate desserts or

Hot Chocolate

Include a flask to drink from (make believe he or she is skiing in the Alps); white and red napkins.

HAWAIIAN DAY

Barbecued Teriyaki Spareribs

Pineapple Fruit Spears

Banana-Snow Pea Crunches

Fruit Punch or a whole coconut (drill a small hole in it—it won't leak—and pack a straw)

Include a paper lei; a sticker of a ukulele; a postcard of Hawaii (or white sand and water) with a message on it; plastic drink stirrer with a palm tree (available in party stores).

FRENCH DAY

Any sandwich on a croissant or

A grilled ham and cheese sandwich (which is a favorite French dish called Croque Monsieur)

Lemon Squares

Colors are red, white and blue so stick to the theme; if you have a beret, pack it, too.

MIDDLE EAST DAY

Esther's Falafel and Hummus Sylvia

Sesame Bars

Anything in a pita bread

Choose a flag and coordinate the colors (for example, Israel is blue and white). If you have a postcard of a camel or a pyramid, include it with a coded message.

ITALIAN DAY

Alice Waters's Pasta Salad

Italian Bread or Simple Cheese Pizza

Ellen's Thumbprint Cookies (decorate with green, red and white sprinkles)

MEXICAN DAY

Guacamole Tacos or

Chicken Fajita Pita

Crunchy Salad

Tortilla Chips

Green Pepper Rods

Spanish Corn Bread

INDIAN DAY

Soft bread (a warmed-up pita will do)

If your child likes curry, make the Curried Shredded Wheat snack

Chutney

Indian Peanut Dip or anything with peanuts

Yogurt with sliced cucumbers

The Perfect Pantry

Having the perfect pantry is easy. All it takes is keeping your cabinets, pantry and refrigerator stocked with enough foods and ingredients—whether fresh, prepared or dry—so you can make a variety of menus for your child's lunches during the week without making any extra trips to the market. By stocking your kitchen with these items, you will be able to make nearly all of these recipes at the drop of a wide-eyed request. Note that you may want to get some ingredients like avocados (for guacamole) only when you plan to make that particular recipe.

Useful Foods to Always Have in Your Kitchen

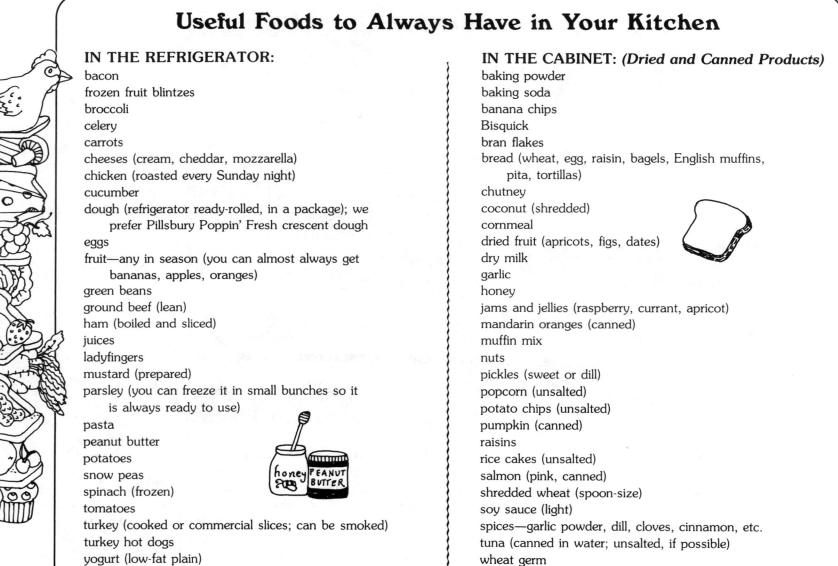

IN THE REFRIGERATOR:

bacon
frozen fruit blintzes
broccoli
celery
carrots
cheeses (cream, cheddar, mozzarella)
chicken (roasted every Sunday night)
cucumber
dough (refrigerator ready-rolled, in a package); we
    prefer Pillsbury Poppin' Fresh crescent dough
eggs
fruit—any in season (you can almost always get
    bananas, apples, oranges)
green beans
ground beef (lean)
ham (boiled and sliced)
juices
ladyfingers
mustard (prepared)
parsley (you can freeze it in small bunches so it
    is always ready to use)
pasta
peanut butter
potatoes
snow peas
spinach (frozen)
tomatoes
turkey (cooked or commercial slices; can be smoked)
turkey hot dogs
yogurt (low-fat plain)

IN THE CABINET: *(Dried and Canned Products)*

baking powder
baking soda
banana chips
Bisquick
bran flakes
bread (wheat, egg, raisin, bagels, English muffins,
    pita, tortillas)
chutney
coconut (shredded)
cornmeal
dried fruit (apricots, figs, dates)
dry milk
garlic
honey
jams and jellies (raspberry, currant, apricot)
mandarin oranges (canned)
muffin mix
nuts
pickles (sweet or dill)
popcorn (unsalted)
potato chips (unsalted)
pumpkin (canned)
raisins
rice cakes (unsalted)
salmon (pink, canned)
shredded wheat (spoon-size)
soy sauce (light)
spices—garlic powder, dill, cloves, cinnamon, etc.
tuna (canned in water; unsalted, if possible)
wheat germ
wheat pretzels

READY-MADE SNACKS:

Obviously, the most nutritious (and simplest) snack to include in the lunch box is a piece of fruit. Depending on the season, you can buy apples, bananas, cantaloupe, various berries, grapes, pears, peaches, papaya and so forth. Get your child used to thinking of fruit as a treat so that his or her first choice for a lunch "dessert" will be papaya rather than M&Ms.

However, there are commercial foods available that your child may like that are delicious, relatively nutritious and attractive. These include the following:

almond cookies
alphabet biscuits
dates, apricots, apples and other dried fruit
fig Newtons
fortune cookies

freeze-dried peaches, bananas or banana chips
fruit leathers (look for Fruit Tannery brand, which is
    made without preservatives and comes in many
    flavors)
graham crackers
granola bars
nuts
oatmeal cookies
popcorn (plain, no salt)
potato, corn, tortilla, banana chips
sunflower seeds (shelled)
trail mix (nuts, raisins, seeds)
unsalted wheat pretzels
yogurt-covered raisins or plain raisins

Utensils *(other than your basic kitchen equipment):*

cheese slicer
cookie cutters galore—for breads: large, any
    shape, as many as you can buy; small for
    meats and cheeses
egg slicer
food processor or blender
grater
loaf pans—for baking breads; they come in
    miniature sizes, too, for making several breads
    that can be frozen

measuring cups
measuring spoons
mixing bowls
muffin tin (regular and corn-stick shaped)
rolling pin
skewers—wooden or bamboo, with sharp ends
    broken off
toothpicks

NUTRITIONAL CONTENTS OF OUR RECIPES

MILK PRODUCTS

1 cup plain yogurt
   145 calories
   12 g protein
   415 mg calcium
   326 mg phosphorus
   115 mg sodium
   531 mg potassium
   150 units vitamin A

Cheddar cheese—1-ounce wedge
   115 calories
   7 g protein
   204 mg calcium
   some potassium
   300 units vitamin A

2 tablespoons cream cheese
   100 calories
   2 g protein
   23 mg calcium
   71 mg potassium
   400 units vitamin A

1 hard-cooked egg
   80 calories
   6 g protein
   28 mg calcium
   61 mg sodium
   65 mg potassium
   260 units vitamin A

1 tablespoon soft margarine
   100 calories
   3 mg calcium
   140 mg sodium
   470 units vitamin A

FISH

1 ounce fish stick (fresh fish)
   50 calories
   5 g protein
   3 mg calcium

3 ounces pink salmon
   120 calories
   17 g protein
   167 mg calcium
   243 mg phosphorus
   580 mg sodium
   307 mg potassium
   60 units vitamin A

1 cup tuna salad (made with
   celery, mayonnaise,
   onion and egg)
   350 calories
   30 g protein
   41 mg calcium
   270 mg phosphorus
   430 mg sodium
   590 units vitamin A

MEATS AND POULTRY

3 ounces very lean ground beef
   185 calories
   23 g protein
   10 mg calcium
   57 mg sodium
   261 mg potassium
   20 units vitamin A

3 ounces lean roast beef
   165 calories
   25 g protein
   11 mg calcium
   208 mg phosphorus
   3+ mg iron
   279 mg potassium
   10 units vitamin A

2 slices fried bacon
   85 calories
   4 g protein
   2 mg calcium
   35 mg phosphorus
   153 mg sodium

3 ounces ham
   245 calories
   18 g protein
   8 mg calcium
   145 mg phosphorus
   271 mg sodium
   199 mg potassium

1 slice lunch meat (ham)
   65 calories
   5 g protein
   3 mg calcium
   400 mg sodium

1 chicken drumstick
   88 calories
   12 g protein
   6 mg calcium
   90 mg phosphorus

2 slices white meat turkey
   150 calories
   28 g protein
   3.8 mg iron
   70 mg sodium
   350 mg potassium
   9 mg niacin

1 hot dog
   170 calories
   7 g protein
   3 mg calcium
   57 mg phosphorus

1 slice salami
   45 calories
   2 g protein
   3 mg calcium
   180 mg sodium
   28 mg phosphorus
   traces of vitamins B_1 & B_2

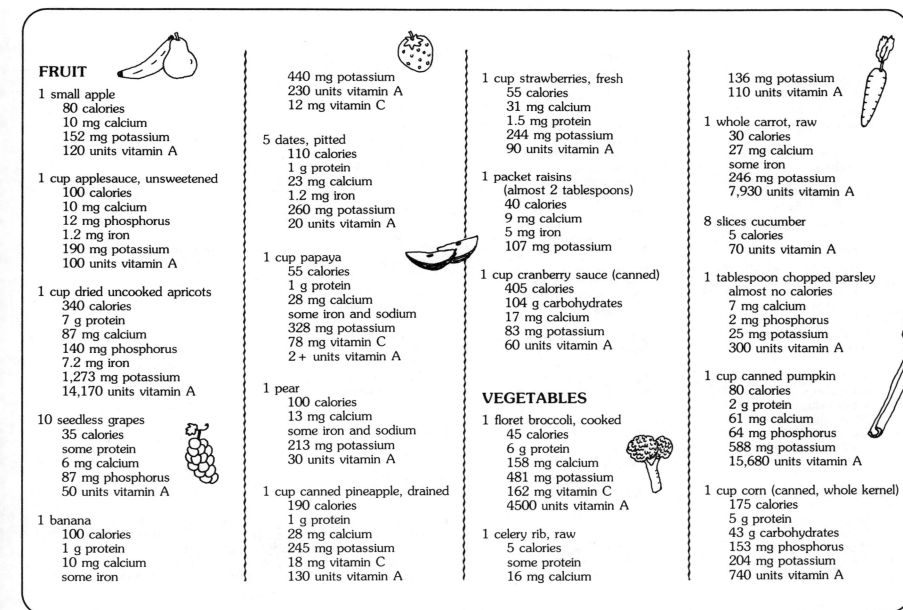

FRUIT

1 small apple
  80 calories
  10 mg calcium
  152 mg potassium
  120 units vitamin A

1 cup applesauce, unsweetened
  100 calories
  10 mg calcium
  12 mg phosphorus
  1.2 mg iron
  190 mg potassium
  100 units vitamin A

1 cup dried uncooked apricots
  340 calories
  7 g protein
  87 mg calcium
  140 mg phosphorus
  7.2 mg iron
  1,273 mg potassium
  14,170 units vitamin A

10 seedless grapes
  35 calories
  some protein
  6 mg calcium
  87 mg phosphorus
  50 units vitamin A

1 banana
  100 calories
  1 g protein
  10 mg calcium
  some iron

  440 mg potassium
  230 units vitamin A
  12 mg vitamin C

5 dates, pitted
  110 calories
  1 g protein
  23 mg calcium
  1.2 mg iron
  260 mg potassium
  20 units vitamin A

1 cup papaya
  55 calories
  1 g protein
  28 mg calcium
  some iron and sodium
  328 mg potassium
  78 mg vitamin C
  2+ units vitamin A

1 pear
  100 calories
  13 mg calcium
  some iron and sodium
  213 mg potassium
  30 units vitamin A

1 cup canned pineapple, drained
  190 calories
  1 g protein
  28 mg calcium
  245 mg potassium
  18 mg vitamin C
  130 units vitamin A

1 cup strawberries, fresh
  55 calories
  31 mg calcium
  1.5 mg protein
  244 mg potassium
  90 units vitamin A

1 packet raisins
  (almost 2 tablespoons)
  40 calories
  9 mg calcium
  5 mg iron
  107 mg potassium

1 cup cranberry sauce (canned)
  405 calories
  104 g carbohydrates
  17 mg calcium
  83 mg potassium
  60 units vitamin A

VEGETABLES

1 floret broccoli, cooked
  45 calories
  6 g protein
  158 mg calcium
  481 mg potassium
  162 mg vitamin C
  4500 units vitamin A

1 celery rib, raw
  5 calories
  some protein
  16 mg calcium

  136 mg potassium
  110 units vitamin A

1 whole carrot, raw
  30 calories
  27 mg calcium
  some iron
  246 mg potassium
  7,930 units vitamin A

8 slices cucumber
  5 calories
  70 units vitamin A

1 tablespoon chopped parsley
  almost no calories
  7 mg calcium
  2 mg phosphorus
  25 mg potassium
  300 units vitamin A

1 cup canned pumpkin
  80 calories
  2 g protein
  61 mg calcium
  64 mg phosphorus
  588 mg potassium
  15,680 units vitamin A

1 cup corn (canned, whole kernel)
  175 calories
  5 g protein
  43 g carbohydrates
  153 mg phosphorus
  204 mg potassium
  740 units vitamin A

1 dill pickle
   5 calories
   17 mg calcium
   920 mg sodium
   130 mg potassium
   170 units vitamin A

3 slices tomato (½ tomato)
   12 calories
   8 mg calcium
   16 mg phosphorus
   150 mg potassium
   550 units vitamin A

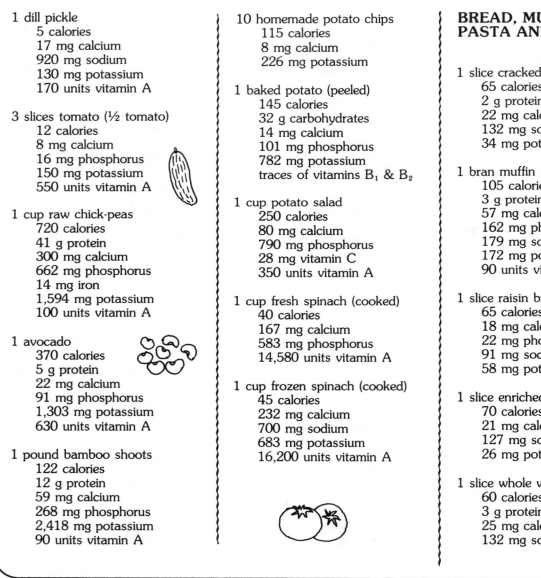

1 cup raw chick-peas
   720 calories
   41 g protein
   300 mg calcium
   662 mg phosphorus
   14 mg iron
   1,594 mg potassium
   100 units vitamin A

1 avocado
   370 calories
   5 g protein
   22 mg calcium
   91 mg phosphorus
   1,303 mg potassium
   630 units vitamin A

1 pound bamboo shoots
   122 calories
   12 g protein
   59 mg calcium
   268 mg phosphorus
   2,418 mg potassium
   90 units vitamin A

10 homemade potato chips
   115 calories
   8 mg calcium
   226 mg potassium

1 baked potato (peeled)
   145 calories
   32 g carbohydrates
   14 mg calcium
   101 mg phosphorus
   782 mg potassium
   traces of vitamins B_1 & B_2

1 cup potato salad
   250 calories
   80 mg calcium
   790 mg phosphorus
   28 mg vitamin C
   350 units vitamin A

1 cup fresh spinach (cooked)
   40 calories
   167 mg calcium
   583 mg phosphorus
   14,580 units vitamin A

1 cup frozen spinach (cooked)
   45 calories
   232 mg calcium
   700 mg sodium
   683 mg potassium
   16,200 units vitamin A

BREAD, MUFFINS, PASTA AND CEREALS

1 slice cracked wheat bread
   65 calories
   2 g protein
   22 mg calcium
   132 mg sodium
   34 mg potassium

1 bran muffin
   105 calories
   3 g protein
   57 mg calcium
   162 mg phosphorus
   179 mg sodium
   172 mg potassium
   90 units vitamin A

1 slice raisin bread
   65 calories
   18 mg calcium
   22 mg phosphorus
   91 mg sodium
   58 mg potassium

1 slice enriched white bread
   70 calories
   21 mg calcium
   127 mg sodium
   26 mg potassium

1 slice whole wheat bread
   60 calories
   3 g protein
   25 mg calcium
   132 mg sodium

1 egg bagel
   165 calories
   6 g protein
   95 mg sodium
   55 mg potassium

1 corn muffin
   125 calories
   3 g protein
   42 mg calcium
   68 mg phosphorus
   54 mg potassium
   120 units vitamin A

1 hamburger or hot dog bun
   120 calories
   3 g protein
   30 mg calcium
   34 mg phosphorus
   202 mg sodium
   38 mg potassium

1 cup cornmeal (about 6 ounces)
   435 calories
   12 g protein
   129 g carbohydrates
   24 mg calcium
   310 mg phosphorus
   2.9 mg iron
   346 mg potassium
   620 units vitamin A

1 slice cheese pizza
   145 calories
   6 g protein
   22 g carbohydrates
   86 mg calcium

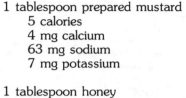

300 mg sodium
67 mg potassium
230 units vitamin A

1 cup cooked pasta
155 calories
5 g protein
32 g carbohydrates
11 mg calcium
70 mg phosphorus
85 mg potassium

1 cup bran cereal
105 calories
4 g protein
19 mg calcium
125 mg phosphorus
15.6 mg iron
137 mg potassium
1,650 units vitamin A

1 cup shredded wheat (spoon-size)
90 calories
2 g protein
11 mg calcium
97 mg phosphorus

COOKIES AND SNACKS

4 fig bars
200 calories
2 g protein

141 mg sodium
111 mg potassium
60 units vitamin A

¼ cup slivered almonds
165 calories
5 g protein
225 mg potassium
traces of vitamins B$_1$ & B$_2$

1 tablespoon peanut butter
95 calories
4 g protein
9 mg calcium
61 mg phosphorus
97 mg sodium
100 mg potassium

1 cup roasted and salted peanuts
840 calories
37 g protein
107 mg calcium
577 mg phosphorus
3 mg iron
602 mg sodium
971 mg potassium
traces of vitamins B$_1$ & B$_2$

4 oatmeal cookies with raisins
235 calories
3 g protein
11 mg calcium
84 mg sodium

192 mg potassium
30 units vitamin A

½ cup dried sunflower seeds
400 calories
17 g protein
85 mg calcium
600 mg phosphorus
5 mg iron
650 mg potassium
35 units vitamin A
traces of vitamins B$_1$ & B$_2$

MISCELLANEOUS FOODS

1 ounce unsweetened
baking chocolate
1.3 calories
2 + g protein
16 mg calcium
81 mg phosphorus
174 mg potassium
10 units vitamin A

1 tablespoon mayonnaise
100 calories
11 g fat
3 mg calcium
84 mg sodium
40 units vitamin A

1 tablespoon prepared mustard
5 calories
4 mg calcium
63 mg sodium
7 mg potassium

1 tablespoon honey
55 calories
trace of protein,
thiamin and vitamin C
17 g carbohydrates
11 mg potassium

Information condensed from U.S. Department of Agriculture *Handbook on Nutritional Contents of Common Foods*.

INDEX

*An asterisk following a recipe title indicates that that recipe should be prepared in advance.